DARKNESS
in PARADISE

Memories of ~~Gloria VanDemmeltr~~aadt
From His Youth ~~in Indonesia D~~uring WWII

Gloria VanDemmeltraadt

Editing and proofreading by Charlene Roemhildt, Meg Corrigan, and Connie Anderson

Cover photo by Gloria VanDemmeltraadt

Back cover photo of Gloria and Onno: Used with permission from ©Lifetouch, Inc.

Archway Publishing books may be ordered through booksellers or by contacting:

Archway Publishing
1663 Liberty Drive
Bloomington, IN 47403
www.archwaypublishing.com
1 (888) 242-5904

ISBN: 978-1-4808-1539-1 (sc)
ISBN: 978-1-4808-1540-7 (e)

Library of Congress Control Number: 2015901862

Printed in the United States of America.

Archway Publishing rev. date: 02/11/2015

Reproduced with permission from the Lonely Planet website
www.lonelyplanet.com © 2014 Lonely Planet.

Table of Contents

Preface

How and why this story came about

There have been thousands of books and articles written about World War II and its worldwide effects. However, in the U.S. particularly, I've learned there isn't much information about Indonesia in the history books. At my family's urging, I decided to capture my own memories of growing up in Indonesia during the war, and of living in Holland as well.

Many documents portray the WWII years as only gloom and doom, and with no question it was a terrible period of hardship and suffering for my family and for millions of others. I want to also share memories of a happy childhood in beautiful and lush surroundings in the country of my birth. The Dutch East Indies, as it was known at that time, was paradise to me.

For the most part, my memories are upbeat and happy because that is my nature, which I believe I inherited from my father. Even under dire circumstances I have always found, as he did, there is something to laugh about as well as to learn from. The experiences and lessons learned, and more so the caring environment provided by loving parents, brother, aunts, uncles, and cousins, helped instill in me a confident and optimistic view for a happy future.

Above all else, as demonstrated by my mother, there was unwavering faith in a loving God's protection and guidance, which continues to bring me peace.

My heartfelt gratitude goes out to my wife Gloria. Without her talent, tenacity, and insistence to put my story on paper, it would never have happened. Thank you Gloria, for helping me put my memories in writing.

Thank you to my children, Mark and Jennifer, for your motivation and support, and also to my extended family for blessing further chapters in my life. These chapters begin where this story ends, with my move to the United States in 1961 along with my first wife Marjanne, who passed away in 2003. Perhaps one day these chapters will be documented as well.

I fully understand that everyone has different memories of the same events, depending on how we see the world. This story is told from my perspective, as truthfully and clearly as I can make it. If it is different from the memories of others who lived the same events, I can only say that I hope to hear your version someday.

Throughout the document, some names have been changed because it is not possible to locate descendants of some of the people whose stories I tell. All of the stories are vital to the collective whole, and if some names are not familiar to those who shared my past, there is a reason.

May you enjoy this story as much as I have enjoyed bringing it to you, and may God continue to bless us all.

Onno VanDemmeltraadt

Introduction

Early history of my fatherland

As early as the 14th and 15th centuries, explorers from different nations traveled the world in search of new territories to exploit for trading purposes. Trading companies in the Netherlands focused their attention primarily on the Far East. Southeast of Malaysia, west of the nation of Papua New Guinea, northwest of Australia, and bordered by the Indian Ocean in the west and the Pacific in the east, they discovered an enormous tropical island paradise. It was the world's largest archipelagic collection of isles, consisting of 18,110 islands rich in oil, tin, copra (the dried kernel of the coconut used to extract coconut oil) and spices. The region also was an important trade route to China, thriving in trade of spices. Initially, the Dutch traders settled only on Java, the most densely populated island. Over the centuries, they increased their influence, establishing an army and gradually placing the whole archipelago under its authority. They called the new colony The Dutch East Indies.[1]

Prior to 1800, the VOC*, the Dutch trading company, dealt mainly in sugar and tea. It had plantations all around the islands that are now known as Indonesia, and had a great deal of power

[1] Sjoerd A. Lapré, RMWO, *Nederlands-Indie 1940-1950 In Kort Bestek*. Permission received through Ronny Herman de Jong and her book *Rising from the Shadow of the Sun*.

in the country. The VOC, however, went bankrupt in 1800 and ceased to exist. There was French involvement at this time, too, when Napoleon occupied the Netherlands, and even under the French, the Dutch continued to colonize the Dutch East Indies.

*From Wikipedia®, The Dutch East India Company (Dutch: Vereenigde Oost-Indische Compagnie, VOC, "United East India Company") was a chartered company established in 1602, when the States-General of the Netherlands granted it a 21-year monopoly to carry out colonial activities in Asia. It is often considered to have been the first multinational corporation in the world and it was the first company to issue stock. It was also arguably the first megacorporation, possessing quasi-governmental powers, including the ability to raise an army (of conscripted soldiers, not forced) to wage war, imprison and execute convicts, negotiate treaties, coin money, and establish colonies.

Statistically, the VOC eclipsed all of its rivals in the Asia trade. Between 1602 and 1796 the VOC sent almost a million Europeans to work in the Asia trade on 4,785 ships, and netted for their efforts more than 2.5 million tons of Asian trade goods. By contrast, the rest of Europe combined sent only 882,000 people from 1500 to 1795, and the fleet of the English (later British) East India Company, the VOC's nearest competitor, was a distant second to its total traffic with 2,690 ships and a mere one-fifth the tonnage of goods carried by the VOC. The VOC enjoyed huge profits from its spice monopoly through most of the 17th century.

After the VOC, there eventually came another Dutch company, called HVA, which stood for Handelsverengiging Amsterdam. This trading company was established in 1873. The HVA was instrumental in the Dutch East Indies in cultivation of sugar cane, coffee, cassava and sisal. It was once one of the largest colonial companies in the world, and in 1928 they had 36 companies and 170,000 workers in the Dutch East Indies.

The spice trade was a large part of the activities of both the VOC and the HVA, as there are specific spices that grow on certain islands that are valuable all over the world. This led to the early name of "The Spice Islands," by which the entire area was once known. For example, cloves, nutmeg, and mace grow only on a few islands in Indonesia. There are also cinnamon, turmeric, vanilla, ginger, and cardamom, which is in the ginger family, plus of course, the sugar, coffee, and tea plantations on Java, Sumatra, Borneo, Bali, and other islands. In all, there are more than 18,000 islands, thousands of them small and uninhabited, which make up the whole of what is now Indonesia.

Having been set up in 1602, to profit from the Malukan spice trade, in 1619 the VOC established a capital in the port city of Jayakarta and changed the city name to Batavia (now Jakarta). Over the next two centuries the company acquired additional ports as trading bases and safeguarded their interests by taking over surrounding territory. It remained an important trading concern and paid shareholders an 18 percent annual dividend for almost 200 years.

Weighed down by corruption in the late 17th century, the company went bankrupt and was formally dissolved in 1800, its possessions and the debt being taken over by the government of the Dutch Batavian Republic. The VOC's territories became the Dutch East Indies and were expanded over the course of the 19th century to include the whole of the Indonesian archipelago, and in the 20th century would form the Independent Republic of Indonesia.

The independence which is alluded to was claimed in August 1945, but was not official until 1949. Chapter 3, The Bersiap, explains this further.

Developing the land

Originally, only the ports or cities in the Dutch East Indies close to the sea were developed and colonized by the Dutch government to carry on its spice trade. Jakarta was one of the first ports on the west side of the island of Java, and Surabaya on the east. Eventually the Dutch saw the need to open the backlands of the islands, and for that they needed to go into the wilderness and build roads. This was a huge move forward in developing the country. According to Wikipedia®, the Dutch East Indies colonial government, from 1810 to 1825, designed and built the De Groote Postweg, or Great Post Road stretching 1,000 kilometers (about 622 miles) from west of Jakarta to East Java near Surabaya on the eastern coast.

This was an enormous undertaking, with the mountains, volcanoes, and jungles all through the island. Surabaya is at sea level and is hot and humid, but farther up in the mountains it is cooler and more bearable, so the road-building might have been a little easier. This is a good area for the plantations, and the road opened up possibilities for plantations which produced sugar, coffee, tobacco, and tea, as well as spice plantations.

The main representative of the Dutch government in Indonesia was called the Governor General, and he was the head of the business or organization which took over after the demise of the VOC.

As Dutch school children in the Dutch East Indies we were taught that this colonial government was wonderful and they built the road that opened up the interior of Java, and accomplished all sorts of advances for the country. In reality, these people were brutal. For example, they used local people from the villages to build the road along the way. Here is my understanding of how it came about:

The bosses of the project would go to a village and say to the village mayor, "Assign 15 or 20 men to do the work, and your responsibility is to build the road from this point to that point." They'd go to the next village and tell them the same thing. Of course, the villagers were not accustomed to building roads; their daily routine was planting rice and making a living for their families. There was probably a little training involved, but soon the diplomats went away and left the workers to build the road.

The diplomats came back in a couple of months to see the people had accomplished only a minor percentage of the work to be done. The bosses listened to the people's excuses of so and so getting sick, or having too much to do, or whatever. The bosses then told them to find others who were not sick or too busy and have them do the work. In addition they said, "Because you didn't get the work done, now you have to do an extra half mile."

When the bosses came back after another three months, the people were only 50 percent done with the original amount of the work. They had more excuses that the children had been sick, there was not enough food, and so on. So the leader of the bosses said to his sergeant, "See that high tree over there? Go get the mayor of the village and hang the man."

The sergeant did what he was told and there was a public hanging of the mayor. Then the leader turned in his saddle to the man who was second in command of the village. He said to him, "Now you are the mayor of the village. It is your responsibility to complete the work which has been assigned from here to there, plus you have another half mile."

Not surprisingly, three months later the work was done.

Ultimately, this helped all of the people in opening the country for better use of the land, but at great cost. While the work got done, it was done in a brutal way.

Java is only one of more than 18,000 islands of Indonesia, but it was the first to be colonized and developed. For reasons unknown to me, the Javanese through the ages have been the dominant class among the natives. Eventually, many or most of the other islands were colonized in a similar way. Sumatra, for example, is much larger than Java, but it was colonized later.

All of the native people in Indonesia are extremely superstitious and as such, seem to be easily led. The Javanese were more advanced than other tribes in their culture and legends, and they became the most powerful and influential. However, they, too, seemed to easily succumb to the influence of Europeans.

Companies and businesses like sugar and spice plantations were usually led by Dutch or European men. In the 1700s, the VOC military had been sent to colonize the area, establish law and order, and launch local government. Eventually, these men married or lived with local women and had children.

Dutch Names

Dutch family surnames were not required until after Napoleon annexed the Netherlands in 1811.[2] Napoleon Bonaparte became the leader of France after the revolution at the end of the 1700s, and conquered half of Europe as well, including Holland in the early 1800s. Along the way, Napoleon decided all people needed to be registered, and in order to do that everyone had to have a surname. In those days, only nobility or upper class people had two names, and most common people went by only one.

Not everyone was happy about having to come up with a surname now that they were forced to do it. People determined that most any name would do, and they often named themselves according to their trade or profession, like Baker, Timmerman (which means carpenter), or Boer (farmer). They also used the name of their town. After that came adding the term 'son' to the name to indicate the next generation, like Bakerson. Also, many people thought the naming thing was not serious or permanent, and they named themselves humorous names like nicknames.

A man I knew from Zandvoort, a village in Holland, had a name that had carried on through generations, and when I was a young boy, this man named Penis drove a cart through the city selling fruit-ice, like Popsicles, with his name prominently displayed on his cart. This was enough to give all of us young boys fits of giggles whenever we saw him.

The name VanDemmeltraadt originally came from Germany. My family has traced it back to the 1700s. The name came from a town

---

[2] Schulze, Lorine McGinnis (2008-03-04). "Dutch Patronymics of the 1600s." *New Netherland, New York Genealogy*. Olive Tree Genealogy.

called Demmel in Germany which was close to the Dutch border. "Van" means "from" or "of" and I know the city council is called "Raad," and one of the first van Demmeltraadts was a member of the city council in Amsterdam. I think that's how the name developed, but it all gets pretty confusing. At first the "van" was considered not important and it wasn't capitalized, and was also separated by a space from Demmeltraadt. For example, in one of my father's many photographs of motorcycle racing, he had a big "D" on his helmet, which shows that the "van" was not an important part of his name. Actually, in Holland the name is still spelled that way. The name eventually became "Americanized," when I decided to capitalize the van, attach it to the rest of the name and it became VanDemmeltraadt. This happened after my U.S. naturalization in 1967.

The Netherlands/Holland

To avoid confusion throughout this narrative, it is important to clarify use of the terms "Netherlands" and "Holland." While the formal name of the country is the Netherlands, most Dutch people and many others refer to the whole country as Holland (even the country's website is called Holland.com). The Netherlands is a country comprised of 12 provinces, two of which are North Holland and South Holland. The majority of the population of the country lives in these two provinces and this may have contributed to the popularity of calling the country Holland. In any case, it should be noted when I mention Holland in this document, I am referring to the Netherlands.

My family's roots

My grandfather, Pieter Antonie van Demmeltraadt, was full Dutch. He was born in Utrecht, Holland, in the 1870s before the family moved to Amsterdam. His father was an alcoholic and the man abused his wife. When young Pieter was 17 he could stand it no more, and one day when his father was beating his mother, he grabbed the man and threw him down the steps. After that he was thrown out of the house. With nothing else to do, he signed up for the army of the Dutch colony in the East Indies. Young men got a certain amount of money to sign up for this service, so it was a way for them to support themselves, and it was also quite exciting and a little glamorous for them in the beginning.

Yes, the Dutch and other Europeans went "directly" to the Dutch East Indies to colonize the area and serve in the army. However, getting there was not as "direct" as one might think. It was a long journey from the Netherlands to the Dutch East Indies, and with no modern transportation, the only way to get there was to go by ship around the Cape of Good Hope, in South Africa. There was no Suez Canal in those days.

It was a terribly long ocean voyage and they ran out of food and good water and people got sick from lack of vitamins and vegetables and fruits. The journey took many months and any glamour there was in the beginning about the trip wore off quickly.

As a result of the tortuous voyage, the Dutch made settlements in South Africa to provide fresh food and provisions for the ships so they could continue their journey. These settlements grew and were colonies of the Dutch as far back as the 1600s until around 1800 when the South African colonies were wrested away by the British.

As the VOC grew in the Dutch East Indies, it began to develop its own small army to defend their settlements from rivals such as Spain, Portugal, England, and other countries, for the valuable spice trade.

Initially, the VOC made trade agreements with the natives. The Europeans began to fight each other and they bribed the local princes to get their monopolies. Then those princes and warlords and potentates sometimes played a double role and they created their own little armies to enforce their treaties. The army started by the VOC began to grow and it was primarily made up of young Dutch boys like my grandfather.

I recently learned that to get more soldiers for their army, the

VOC actually bought 4,000 slaves in Africa in the early days. The slaves signed a contract for four years and after they fulfilled their time, they would be free people. This was a pretty attractive offer and many of them served their time and fought for the VOC and afterwards stayed in the East Indies.

These people who started in slavery and were then trained as soldiers, were big strong men, extremely fierce, and extremely feared in this gentle country which had never seen men such as they. Native women, however, conquered their fear and intermarried with these African men, and did likewise with the Europeans.

In Indonesia, there are many black descendants from the original African slaves. There are also the Ambonese from the Indonesian island of Ambon, who are dark skinned. The Ambonese could be related to the Papua from New Guinea, or even the Australian Aborigines, and they have a distinctly different look. As mentioned, there are thousands of small islands throughout Indonesia, and most of the people are quite distinctive according to where they were born.

For example, on the island of Java, where I lived, there is the province of West Java where the people are called Sundanese, and East Java where they are called Javanese, and Central Java, which has a mixture of people. Java is the most populated of all the Indonesian islands, but it is not the largest. The people of West Java are lighter skinned and more slender than the Javanese, who are more stocky and muscular. In addition, their languages are completely different. The Javanese are a more formal people and their dress is dark. The Sundanese wear brighter colors and are more forward and outgoing, and are eager to talk.

I believe my father's mother was a descendent of one of the African slaves. She could have been part European, English most likely and part African. She was quite dark skinned, but had light blue eyes. Her name was Josephine Hooper, and family memories say my Dutch grandfather met her at a dance. They ultimately married and had two sons. My uncle, Joop, and my father, Frits, were fairly light skinned and both had blue eyes.

My father's full name was Frits Eduard Maximiliaan van Demmeltraadt, and I tell more of his story in following chapters. Oom (Dutch for Uncle) Joop (Johannes Josephus Marinus van Demmeltraadt) stayed in Indonesia until all the Dutch were thrown out in 1956 (explained in Chapter 6). He married a girl of mixed native and European descent, and they had three children; Yvonne, called Onnie, Pieter, and Marijke.

My grandfather Pieter van Demmeltraadt served his time in the Dutch East Indies Army and he stayed in the East Indies. He lived in Surabaya, on the far eastern end of Java. This was and is a hot tropical climate, yet he wore a three-piece suit with a tie every day. He worked with a company which had sugar mills and a plantation, and was part of the HVA. He was a secretary for the company, like an executive officer, which was an important position.

Figure 1 My maternal grandfather, Bernhard Ernst Gustav Guisbert Schmidt, early 1900s. Photographer unknown.

My maternal grandfather followed a similar course as the young Pieter van Demmeltraadt. Bernhard Ernst Gustav Guisbert Schmidt grew up in a good home in Prussia, and they had a lot of property. The reason isn't known, but it is understood that he was forced to leave home as a young man, about 16 or 17 years old, and he ended up in Rotterdam, which was the big harbor and sea port of the Netherlands. He, too, joined the army of the Dutch East Indies and went to Indonesia.

Both of these men ended up as Sergeant Majors in the army, both were sharp-shooters, and both were classified as being masters at all weapons. This would have been in the late 1800s.

With the sum of money received when he got out of the army, my German grandfather Schmidt acquired property around a lake and he developed it into a resort. This small village was called Wendit, near the city of Malang in East Java. It was not far from Surabaya, and people from there would go to the resort on vacations.

Schmidt was quite ambitious and industrious, and worked hard on his property. Stories were told that the family lived in one tiny cabin at the resort. They had servants to do the work, but the whole family lived in a small cabin. When Grandfather Schmidt added on and built more cabins, he rented those out and the family still lived in a small place. He then bought some canoes and boats and kept on expanding the cabins. He also built a large swimming pool. It was a natural spring with native stone so there was no need for cement or anything. The water went through the pool from a spring going to the lake beyond, so the water was crystal clear but extremely cold.

My father and his family went to the resort at Wendit on their vacations, as did many others, and that was likely how my parents met. I once heard my mother was being courted by my father's brother, Joop, but she decided on Frits instead. Both Frits and Joop were good looking and considered real gentlemen.

There exists a document that records the birth of my mother. It appears that Grandfather Schmidt took up with a Javanese woman named Kasmina (no last name). Kasmina had been born in the *Kraton* or palace in Cirebon, West Java. It is believed that Kasmina could have been the daughter of a king or a prince and his concubine, because we know Kasmina was born in the palace.

Figure 2 Back row left to right: Ben, or Bernhard Fritz Alfred; Berta Corrie Elisabeth; Willy Paul Herman; Marie, or Berta Marie; front row: Erna Coba Anna (my mother); Kasmina; and Maps, or Martha Johanna Wilhelmina. The dog in the photo was a family pet that eventually got in a fight with a panther. He killed the panther, but the dog also died later. This picture was taken at Trawas in approximately 1912 when it appears that my mother was about five years old. Photographer unknown.

In those days, formal marriages were not common between Europeans and native Indonesians, but it was important for them to formally recognize children born to their unions. The document I refer to lists my grandfather's age as 45, and it is loosely translated here:

Today, the 6th of December, of 1907, appeared before me, Eduard Martens, clerk of registrations in Malang,

Bernhard Ernst Gustav Guisbert Schmidt, at the age of 45, of private profession, living in Wendit, a suburb of Malang, and declared the birth of his daughter, in Wendit, September 25, 1907, at 4:00 in the morning, being a female child of the free native woman Kasmina, without profession, and living in Wendit, naming the child Erna Coba Anna. Bernhard Ernst Gustav Guisbert Schmidt declared to recognize the child as his child.

This declaration is done in the presence of mentioned free native woman Kasmina, who as mother of the mentioned child declares to agree with the declaration. Also as witnesses present were Martinus Theodorus van Aalst being an age of 51 years, and Jan Martens, age 25 years.

From which declaration this document was made and after reading it and presenting it in the Indonesian language and signed with the exception of the aforementioned woman, Kasmina, who declared that she could not write, now signed by Bernard Ernst Gustav Guisbert Schmidt, Martinus Theodorus van Aalst, and Jan Martens.

This document was witnessed in Surabaya on August 17, 1914, to recognize the signatures, and was signed by the president of the judicial office in Surabaya, legally binding the relationship of the child to my grandfather.

Before Kasmina was united with my grandfather, she had been married or lived in Malang with another Dutch man named Klaverstein. Kasmina and Klaverstein had a daughter named Mien (who eventually became the mother of my cousins Ina, Hanna, and Peter). Klaverstein was reasonably well-to-do, but he died young. He was concerned that his daughter be brought up well in case something happened to him, and his wife might go back to living in a *kampong* (the term for the local native villages). Klaverstein approached another well-to-do Dutch family friend and gave them the authority to be pseudo-parents to Mien to be sure she would have a Dutch upbringing. Sure enough, Klaverstein did become sick and died young, and Mien was raised by the other Dutch family.

After the death of Klaverstein, instead of going back to the *kampong*, Kasmina met my grandfather, and subsequently had several more children with him, including a boy who died young, plus Marie, Berta, Willy, Ben, my mother Erna Coba Anna, and Martha, called Maps. It isn't known whether there are such legal documents for the other children, but this one for Erna is at least, in my possession.

Whether the Europeans married the native women or not, it was important to the fathers to recognize the children of such unions to ensure they had the opportunity for a good future. In fact, if a couple happened to split after children were born, it was not uncommon for Dutch fathers to take the children to Holland to be educated. Many times, the children never returned to Indonesia, and it is supposed their mothers never saw them again.

It isn't known how or if Kasmina was actually of royal blood. However, there is a story about her that does bond her to the palace or *Kraton* at Ceribon, in West Java. She might have been the daughter of a concubine or someone connected to the king. Kasmina was living with, if not married to my grandfather Schmidt, and they were running their resort on the lake at Wendit. One day Kasmina's brothers came to visit. Their clothing and accessories identified them clearly as people of nobility. As they asked people from the town how to locate their sister, the people they addressed bowed and fell on their knees before they answered. This was a class distinction and a sign of reverence when addressing royalty, and definitely a sign that Kasmina was originally from the palace. I've learned recently that Kasmina and her sister Maktje (both Muslims) had fled the palace when they were young and somehow made their way to East Java where Kasmina eventually met Klaverstein and then Schmidt.

Grandfather Schmidt sold the Wendit property and bought a large house farther up in the mountains at Trawas, which was used as his retirement home. The property was probably about 10 acres, with a lake, and he had cows and a horse. There was no electricity, and they used oil lamps throughout the house. Most of their children were gone from home by that time.

My parents were married at Trawas, and there are pictures of the huge family gathered there for their wedding. My memories include going there once as a young child with all of the Schmidt children and their families, but my grandfather had died by then. It was traditional for many years at Christmas to have all of their children come to Trawas to visit and the whole family gathered together there. However, after my parents moved to Bandung we were not able to go to many of those gatherings.

Figure 3 **Family grouping on the rocks surrounding the pool at Trawas. We are all cousins along with my mother and two of her sisters. Front row, from left: my brother Huibert, Meiske and Olga; Middle row, from left: me in the sailor suit with a bandage on my leg, cousins Hanna, Peter, Twindie, and Ina. Back row, from left: Maudie, Corrie, my mother Erna, Tante Marie, and Tante Berta. Photo approximately 1939. Photographer unknown.**

On the one trip to Trawas I remember taking as a little guy, we stopped to see the resort at Wendit. I was impressed by the lake which was quite large, and there were boats and canoes people used on the lake. I also remember how cold the water was in the pool, but we did take a dip in it. Another significant memory of the trip was seeing the many monkeys around the house and the grounds. These were small gray monkeys called Java monkeys, and they had no fear of people. They were considered obnoxious pests throughout the island because of their large numbers and their pattern of stealing things like shiny objects and food.

When women from the *kampongs* would bring food and other items to sell at the daily market, they carried their goods in bamboo baskets on their heads as they walked along the road. The Java monkeys would lie in wait in the trees and when the women passed by the monkeys would leap onto the baskets and steal their goods. By the time the women could do anything about it or get help, the monkeys were long gone.

In the picture above, both Huibert and I had bandages on our legs. This seemed to be a common occurrence when we were young. In the hot tropical climate of the Dutch East Indies, bacteria flourished, and when we got scrapes or cuts, they became infected easily, and took a long time to heal. We had two types of salve for our injuries: one was a heavy black tar, called igtiol, and the other was a more gentle salve called purol, and both seemed to eventually heal our hurts. Igtiol was a "mean" salve and often left a big crater in the skin when the wound healed. It was used only on bad infections. One time I stepped on a rusty nail that went into my heel. After a few days I saw a red line going up my leg that must have been blood poisoning. My mother applied the igtiol salve and after a long time of difficult healing, the wound finally closed and the red line went away.

Another incident with a bad wound concerns my grandmother. Grandfather Schmidt was an avid hunter, particularly of wild boar. My cousin Corrie tells me that Kasmina had the chore of dealing with the treacherous animals that Schmidt shot. One of them was hanging on a branch waiting for cleaning and Kasmina was accidentally poked in the leg by its fang. The puncture was dangerously deep and according to Corrie, the wound never completely healed, causing Kasmina much agony for the rest of her life.

Indos

In the Dutch East Indies there were many bureaucrats in the government and in the military. Many of the lower positions were filled by natives who were under the supervision of what was called "middle management." Middle management people were usually those of mixed Indonesian and Dutch or European heritage, who were called "Indos."

At first, the name Indo was not a flattering term, particularly to Indos themselves. It wasn't until after WWII when people of mixed descent were kicked out of Indonesia, that the term Indo became more accepted.

Today, there exists a sense of pride in being called Indo. Perhaps this is true for two reasons. First, because it validates one's ancestry and establishes a kinship with both the Dutch or European side, as well as the Indonesian side. Second, it solidifies a connection and substantiates the memories of a country that was truly loved by so many who were forced to leave it.

Chapter 1

My personal story

How my life began

In the 1930s, the Great Depression was felt in the East Indies as it was in the entire world. Prices fell drastically, and it was a crazy time. I remember my mother saying you could buy a bale of refined and processed sugar (100 kilo, or about 200 pounds) for 50 cents. Gasoline went down to three or four cents a liter, and business basically stopped. During this time my parents were married in Situbondo, on the eastern part of the island of Java, in what was then called the Dutch East Indies, where both had been born.

My parents were able to struggle along through most of the Depression, because my father's background was technical, and he had skills that were needed. As a young man, he had been trained as a machinist in a trade school in Surabaya. He worked as an engineer or a machinist in a sugar plantation in Situbondo in East Java, and he was in charge of all the machinery on the plantation.

Harvest time was once a year during the summer months of June, July, or August, and this was the busiest time. The peak time lasted at least a month, and people and machines worked day and night. My father worked with the steam engines to ensure everything worked well to process the sugar cane.

Eventually my father was laid off from his job, as were many others at the time because of the Depression. He may have gotten a little bonus money, but I'm sure it wasn't much.

He then started working for a friend of his in nearby Surabaya in his motorcycle dealership. He worked as a mechanic and may have helped with sales here and there.

Before long, he decided to go on his own, and he became a sort of agent for his friend, who had a big business with Norton Motorcycles. My father moved his small family to the city of Malang, also on the east side of Java, and started selling motorcycles. This was probably at the height of the Depression. I don't know how or why he decided to do it at such a critical point in time, but he started his business in 1933.

My brother Huibert was born March 16, 1932, when our parents lived in Situbondo, and I was born in a hospital in Malang on June 19, 1935.

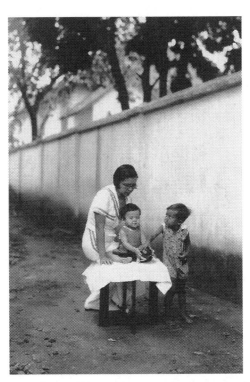

Figure 4 My mother, Erna, with Huibert, age 3, and me as a baby, in late 1935, in Malang, East Java. Photo by Frits van Demmeltraadt, deceased.

Motorcycle racing

In addition to starting his motorcycle business, my father had taken to motorcycle racing in spite of the objections of his father. I have an entire photo album filled with pictures of him racing motorcycles, and still have several of the silver trophies he won.

He started racing when he lived in Malang, and he made quite a name for himself, winning many races. While he still had the shop in Malang, he went to Bandung on the other side of the island of Java, to what must have been a large regional racing event. I once saw a small ad he posted in the Malang newspaper saying the motorcycle shop would be closed while he participated in the races in Bandung. Apparently, he blew everyone away in those regional races, and the newspaper headlines billed him as "the Java Champion."

My brother Huibert says that our father did some work with the army when he was a motorcycle agent in Malang. Eventually, the man he was an agent for was killed in a hunting accident, and there were some problems with another partner who basically swindled the dealership away. Pa, as I always called my father, wanted to get away from this man, and decided to move to Bandung. In Bandung were the headquarters of the Royal Dutch East Indies Army, and he had hopes of doing business with the army there. He moved the family to Bandung and soon opened his own motorcycle dealership. I was only about two years old when my family moved to the other side of the island in 1937.

In Bandung, they raced on a former horse racing track named Tegalega, which was made of grass. Grass could make the track dangerously slippery. Pa built his own racing motorcycle, with an engine ordered from England. The special engine was called a Japp engine, that was 500cc, and he built it in a Rudge frame. It had a gas tank that was flat on the top because he had to lay flat on top of it while racing. He said he was on pins and needles because it had to be shipped from England to the East Indies and he received it only a week before the races would start. He had friends to help him and they worked around the clock on the motorcycle until they had it ready for the big race.

Figure 5 Frits van Demmeltraadt, with the "D" on his helmet (which I still have) after winning a race in 1937 in Bandung, West Java. The man to the left of my father is Joop van Rest, and the man on the far right is Pete Koopman; both also rode motorcycles. Photographer unknown. All in photo are deceased.

When they tried the machine out, it had a lot of power and it was fast, but in the curves the whole combination would shimmy. That, of course, was the last thing you would want – having the bike shimmy in a curve. He tried other tires but in the trial he almost flew out into the hay bales that lined the curve. He worked and worked to solve the shimmying problem, but he just couldn't figure it out. Finally, he decided if he flew off into the *sawas* (rice fields) or hit the bales, so be it. He opened the gas full throttle in the curves giving the engine a lot of juice, which made the motorcycle leap forward. Thus he set off on what could be called a "suicide mission." Remarkably, the machine straightened out and stopped shimmying, and he flew through all of the curves. Whether determined in an emotional instant or a wisely considered decision, the daring option of giving full-throttle seemed to solve the problem. Frits van Demmeltraadt became quite the motorcycle hero of his time.

Figure 6 One of many cartoons in Bandung newspapers depicting my father's motorcycle racing. Pa's number was 1, and he lost a race to #10. Loosely translated, the text of the page is that Demmeltraadt lost only the 350cc race and won everything else. He was consistently called the "Java Champion." Artist P. v. Mierop, deceased.

I was hardly aware of Pa's racing career, being so young, but later in my life I came across many newspaper clippings, photographs, and trophies he won with his daring escapades. Besides the machine he built, there was also a 350cc machine he raced and he did well with that one, too. The bottom line is he knew how to handle a motorcycle.

When Pa was racing, I was allowed to go to the track and sit in the grandstand, called the tribunes, in Bandung. I heard the noise of people talking and the roar of the motorcycles and the dust, but I didn't really know what it was all about. The important thing to me at that time was being allowed to sit in the stands and sip on a small bottle of orange juice, called Green Spot, my favorite treat.

Many times we went home after races to find our house filled with huge wreaths made of flowers and leaves, and there were silver cups, or trophies sitting around. There were many people there congratulating my father. It was quite exciting but as such a tiny child, I didn't fully understand what it was all about.

I know he kept on racing for several years and there is one Bandung news article from 1938 that says F. E. M. van Demmeltraadt was still the Java Champion.

Initially, my father stayed with Norton Motorcycles, which are still built to this day in England. He also began importing others, and sold Harley Davidson, Indian, and BMW motorcycles, plus another German brand of a two-cycle engine called TWN.

The building my father rented in Bandung was originally a residence. It was on the main street or road that went all through the island of Java, as well as through the city of Bandung. It was called De Groote Postweg, or the Great Post Road, and our address was Groote Postweg oost 144. His vision of having his motorcycle shop came true as he converted the front of the house to an office and showroom, and the rest of the house became our home.

Eventually, other businesses were built along that main street. In Bandung, the local natives called the street "Katja Katja Wettan" meaning in Indonesian, "much glass in the west." This was a descriptive way of saying "many glass windows at the west end," because of all the businesses in that area.

Our home

It was comforting to live in the place where my father worked. He wasn't the kind of man to hug me often or pick me up when he saw me, because he was always busy. But he was always there. He was either in the front of the house or working in the back, and it gave me great comfort to know he was there.

In spite of only renting the house, my father made quite a few major changes to it. Besides making the showroom in front, there was another big area in the back he used to repair motorcycles and things. This was a dirty area with oil and grease and tires and all of the tools he needed, but it was big enough for his needs.

Our house was on a normal sized city lot, probably 75 feet wide, but it ran deep. There was no grass in the front and the yard was covered with rocks. Running over those rocks in my bare feet wasn't the most comfortable, but we didn't wear shoes much in those days. My father built a ramp from the front door to the street so he could get motorcycles in and out.

Our house was standard for homes in the East Indies for western or European people. We had a large back yard, and the main house had a number of rooms built on, or attached to the back of it. It was also built several feet above the ground; there was no basement and the built-up floor was solid. I suspect this was to deter snakes or other animals getting into the house. Most houses were only one story, like ours, with high ceilings, which helped to keep the house cool in the tropical climate. Bandung is about 2,100 feet above sea level so it isn't as hot as towns along the coastline. We didn't need electric fans.

The houses of European people and those of more successful native people were built of brick. Most native people lived in what was called a *kampong*, or village, and the houses there were built of bamboo, with roofs made of palm tree leaves.

A European or Indo home had living areas including living rooms and bedrooms for the family and a gallery going away from the house but attached to it, where there were the "smelly areas." These included rooms for gardening equipment, the kitchen, and a number of small rooms where things were stored, like rice and flour, and things like suitcases and items that we in the western world keep in our attics or basements.

The toilets were off this gallery, too, with the toilet area always separated from the bathing area. The bathing room was where you stood and poured water over yourself; there weren't bathtubs as we know them. There was a water reservoir, about three feet square and deep, and you stood beside it and used a dipper to pour water over your soapy body. There was also a shower in the bathroom, but my family preferred to use the Indonesian style of a basin or reservoir and a dipper for washing.

The gallery was covered with a roof, but it was open on one side to the yard. The roof was necessary because of the heavy rainy season, when we had to walk to the toilet and bathroom. Many windows in our house didn't have glass. They were open to the outside, and there were wooden shutters that were closed at night or in bad weather.

There were rooms along the gallery for guests who came from out of town, so they could stay for days or even weeks. There were also rooms for the servants, who normally consisted of a couple who maybe had a child or two. They lived on-site 24 hours a day, and usually the woman was the cook, the most important servant of all, who pretty much told the other servants what to do. The husband of the cook could be a servant also, like a butler, or he could have another job somewhere else and just slept there. Part of the cook's pay was food for herself and her family, plus living quarters.

We had electricity as long as I can remember, and running water and real toilets. The toilets were a luxury as most homes and businesses as well, had only a hole in the floor where people had to squat. This is still true to this day and the restroom stalls in many public buildings have ceramic-lined holes in the floor rather than real toilets as we know them.

Most Europeans and Indos who were half-way up the business ladder had brick houses like ours, with electricity and bathrooms. There were also stoves in the kitchens, most likely gas, or charcoal, as opposed to cooking over an open fire as they did in the *kampongs*.

Household help

Households also had a number of other personnel who worked for the day and went home at night. These were usually native East Indies people who lived elsewhere, perhaps in a *kampong*. There would be a maid for the laundry and one who did the dishes, and one who cleaned the main living quarters, who was called the "indoor maid." There were also people who did the outside work like mowing the lawn and caring for the yard.

The cook had to start very early in the day because there was early breakfast to make, plus *koffie toebroek* to prepare; the strong coffee that is made in individual cups with boiling water. This is a special treat for me to this day and I still have *koffie toebroek* every morning. The main meal of the day was eaten at one o'clock, which required many hours to prepare, so the cook surely did have to start early.

In our house, the main cook was Maktje, my maternal grandmother's sister. Maktje never married and she lived with our family from the time my brother Huibert was born. She was my nursemaid, and in addition, she basically ran the household including the kitchen, and supervised all of the household staff.

Maktje lived first with my mother's older half-sister, *Tante* (Aunt) Mien, and helped with her daughters, Ina and Hanna. Tante Mien's husband, de Vos, died young and she remarried. The story is that Maktje didn't like the new husband and decided to go to our family instead.

Maktje was a native woman, and she did servant duties as the main cook in our household, but she was also family, being my grandmother Kasmina's sister, and she lived with us. I slept in Maktje's room as a tiny boy and most of the time I slept in her bed. The beds in the East Indies then were much bigger than our beds in the U.S. A single bed there was about the size of a queen bed now, so there was plenty of room. This seems odd because the people there are actually quite small and Maktje was a very tiny woman, but that's how it was.

While it was still dark each morning, she would get up and start the cooking fires. When I woke up I stayed with her in the kitchen which was way in the back of the house. The smells of cooking surrounded me like a warm blanket. After breakfast, around nine o'clock or so, Maktje would walk to the market for the food she needed to cook for the day. No words were spoken, but when she got ready to leave, I stood nearby and watched for her finger to reach down. I grabbed ahold of her finger with my right hand, put my left hand thumb in my mouth, and toddled away beside her.

Maktje always dressed in native Javanese costume, and I can remember to this day the comforting smell of her *batik sarong*. Also, she spoke only Javanese. Even though she understood every word of the Dutch language my family used, she never spoke it.

My family believed our house was haunted. I never learned who might be haunting it, but I know that Maktje insisted she had conversations with the male "ghost" who lived there. Sometimes in the night there would be a sound like marbles being thrown on the clay tiles of the roof. This happened many times and no one was ever able to find the source of the sound. My father had some young male friends who sometimes stayed overnight on the weekends. One night the marble-throwing sound happened and the family adults ran out to catch whoever was doing it, thinking it was the young men. There was no one there and no marbles or stones or anything was ever found.

Overall, Indonesia has always had a culture of mystique and witchcraft. In a later chapter, more stories of supernatural events are told.

Early School Days

I have some memories of my early nursery school when I was about four years old. Sometimes Pa brought me to school, and sometimes the house boy put me on the back of his bicycle and he peddled to the school. At the end of the school day one of them picked me up. We played games at school and they were okay, but I found it all a little boring. I did like drawing, but we played with clay and I liked that least of all because it was sticky, and we got dirty fingers. I've never liked to have dirty fingers.

We did make some friends at school, but they lived far away and they were more of Huibert's age than mine. Sometimes they came to our house on their bicycles and eventually Huibert got a bicycle, too, so he could go here and there. I just stayed at home.

I spent a lot of time with Maktje in the kitchen, just watching what she was doing, and I had nice toys. What I liked best were my German army toys, with field artillery and all. The army soldiers all had German helmets, and there were men lying behind machine guns, soldiers manning mortars and cannons, and they were fascinating to play with.

We also had cowboys and horses, made of a gypsum material. My cowboy had a lasso and was about to lasso something. Huibert had a cowboy on a black horse, and I had one on a lighter brown horse. It's odd, but I have always liked light brown horses best. The German soldiers were also made of gypsum. There were toys made out of lead, too, but they were almost flat and only two-dimensional, and the gypsum toys were much more fun.

The cowboy toys came from the U.S., but the best toys in those days came from England. They were little cars, made by Schuco. Some were wind-up things, and others were battery powered. They were small, of course, but very detailed, and I loved to run them all over our floors.

One year on Santa Claus Day, December 5, Santa Claus brought us an electric train. It was fantastic. Pa put everything together and it was going round and round. His brother lived with us at that time, and he put his cigarette in the chimney of the train so it huffed along the track with the chimney smoking. I watched in fascination, but it seemed to be the adults who were playing the most with it. I just sat on the side watching the whole thing. We never did get to play much with the train because it was too complicated for young ones.

Figure 7 Two young brothers proudly display their beautiful Christmas tree in Bandung before the war, 1938. Photo taken by Erna van Demmeltraadt, deceased.

We loved to play cowboys, and I had a gun and holster, which was a little silly on me because I was so little. My gun was almost bigger than I was. I don't really know how we learned to play guns and cowboys, because I never went to any cowboy movies until way after the war. I expect we learned from other kids.

Two movies I saw before the war were starkly memorable. One was "Snow White," and the other "The Wizard of Oz." I liked the music in "Snow White," and loved the dwarfs playing some sort of organ with pistons pumping up and down. Some of the dwarfs were a little scary. Snow White was wonderful, but I was deathly afraid of the witch. "The Wizard of Oz," was scary all the way through, especially the part when the trees were talking and it was dark.

In the theaters in those days, there were men walking around selling treats to the audience. They sold things like drinks and chocolate bars. What we loved best was "Green Spot," the little bottle of orange juice that I mentioned earlier.

My parents didn't read books to us except that my mother often read from the children's Bible. There were beautiful pictures and great stories. The stories about Samson, the strong man were the best. Of course later I learned that Samson was a scoundrel, but he was my hero when I was young.

In 1938 or '39 Oom Joop, my father's brother, and his family moved in with us. There was Oom Joop and Tante Cor, and their three children; Yvonne, Pieter, and Marijke. Marijke was younger than I was and probably about three when they came. Oom Joop also worked in a sugar plantation, as my father had, but in East Java. Pa had lost his job long before Joop did, but eventually Joop lost his job also, due to the world financial crash and the Depression in the 1930s. Joop was also an engineer and Pa believed he could be of help in his motorcycle business, so Oom Joop and his whole family moved in with us.

My cousin Yvonne is five years older than I am which at that time was a huge age difference. I was totally in awe of her in those days. She read me stories and was always teaching me things. The first thing she taught me was to read, and then to write. This was before I started school. In my father's office was a big typewriter, and Yvonne taught me to pick out letters on it. With great hilarity, the first word I learned to type on the typewriter or to write was "poop." In Dutch it is spelled "poep." I rolled in a piece of paper and typed "poep," over and over again to much laughter.

Figure 8 Here I am with the famous "poop machine" behind me. I am obviously very proud and having a wonderful time. Photo taken by Erna van Demmeltraadt, deceased.

On Santa Claus Day, 1939, Santa Claus gave me a huge toy bear. The bear was almost as big as I was. It was a wonderful thing – huge and soft, and it smelled good, and I kept it with me all the time. The bear and I were indivisible; if we had a family picture taken, the bear was in it, and it slept with me every night. It never really had a name; I just called it "Bear." When nursery school started again for my second year, I insisted on taking Bear along to school. I clutched the thing in one arm and sat on the back of the bicycle and the house boy pedaled away and took us both to school.

When I started elementary school, I no longer took the bear to school, but I continued to be carried to school on the bicycle. After our first classes at school, we had a break about ten in the morning. People ordered something to be served to them at break time, and every day I had a cold chocolate milk that was so refreshing. I still remember the comforting taste of that cold chocolate milk.

I went to elementary school about seven-thirty or so, and at one o'clock, school was finished and we all went home for our main meal of the day. We called it our "warm meal," and this was our big *rijsttafel.*[3]

My mother was often sick and many of my memories of her are of when she was having what I now know to be asthma attacks. She struggled for every breath of air, and it was hard to watch her suffer. However, when she was feeling well, I frequently went shopping with her. My mother had beautiful clothes and she had good taste. I don't know why, but she often took me along on shopping trips to department stores and I loved it. When she was trying on clothes in the dressing room, I would find the women's lingerie department, and look for something soft and silky. I'd sit down with my thumb in my mouth and feel the soft silk, and be perfectly content until she was ready to leave. We usually went shopping in the late morning and ended with lunch in a restaurant. We had a nice meal of *gado gado* (salad), or *nasi goring* (fried rice), and had special treats like ice cream afterwards.

In front of our house/motorcycle store was a sidewalk along the street, so there was no real front yard. The street was paved at that time, but it was dusty and dirty with lots of horse droppings because of all the *dokars*, horse drawn carriages. There were a few

---

[3] Wikipedia®: The Indonesian rijsttafel, a Dutch word that literally translates to "rice table," is an elaborate meal adapted by the Indos. It consists of a large number of side dishes served in small portions, accompanied by rice prepared in several different ways. Popular side dishes include egg rolls, sambals (crushed hot peppers), satay, fish, fruit, vegetables, pickles, and nuts. In most areas where it is served, such as the Netherlands, and other areas of heavy Dutch influence (such as parts of the West Indies), it is known under its Dutch name. Although the dishes served are undoubtedly Indonesian, the *rijsttafel*'s origins were colonial. During their presence in Indonesia, the Dutch introduced the rice table not only so they could enjoy a wide array of dishes at a single sitting, but also to impress visitors with the exotic abundance of their colony. *Rijsttafels* strive to feature an array of not only flavors and colors and degrees of spiciness, but also textures, an aspect that is not commonly discussed in Western food. Such textures may include crispy, chewy, slippery, soft, hard, velvety, gelatinous, and runny.

automobiles in those days, and a few more motorcycles, but nothing like that area today, where streets are clogged and completely filled with automobiles and motorcycles, and still a few *dokars*.

People took naps in the afternoon after their big meal, during the heat of the day. Many businesses actually closed in the afternoon while the proprietors napped. I remember standing on the sidewalk with my mother in front of the store, after my nap and a large meal, and feeling very happy. This was something we did often, just standing there watching the sparse traffic go by, and my mother might have been looking for people she knew.

One day she suddenly pointed to the west where the sun was going down. The sky was a brilliant and dazzling shade of red. There were some clouds, but the intense scarlet color spread across the sky like blood running out of an open wound. My mother shuddered and I felt her body tense as I huddled against her, my happiness ebbing away. I can still hear her crying in a frightened voice, "Oh look, how red is the sky! This is a terrible thing – it means war is coming!"

Chapter 2

The War

Before the beginning

Of course there are many horrible stories about World War II; it was unquestionably a terrible time. Tragedies were all around us, but from my child's eye perspective, my view was different. While sometimes my world was scary, it was also intriguing, and sometimes it was downright humorous. I will try to be true to the facts, but this volume is from my view of them.

Before the war, my father was an agent for BMW motorcycles which came from Germany. I often looked longingly in his store's showroom at beautiful glossy magazines which came from Germany. They were filled with propaganda about the German army and Hitler's regime and the Nazis, which of course I couldn't read. The magazines were also filled with pictures of swastikas – fascinating lines that formed an easy-to-draw figure, and I became mesmerized by them.

When I went to nursery school, I liked to draw swastikas and I drew them everywhere – on my books, in clay, on everything. The magazines had pictures of smiling people, racing cars, and the sides of buildings covered with swastikas. Everyone looked so happy and it made me feel good. One day in school I drew a picture I was so proud of. It was a cow I called my "racing cow," and I drew a big swastika on the side of the cow.

This was before the Japanese invasion, but the world was in unrest, and Holland was in friction with Germany. The school became alarmed at my pictures of swastikas and called my parents in to see what I was doing. I'm sure the school was puzzled, but my father understood I had seen the happy people in the magazines, and knew I was merely copying the happiness I saw.

Unfortunately, I kept on drawing swastikas, and if I drew a picture of a house, there would be a big flag on it with a swastika flying. We never knew exactly what happened, but someone from the school must have said something to the police. One day the colonial police came to the motorcycle store and asked my father to go to police headquarters to make a statement about my drawings. He must have convinced them I was harmless, because we didn't have trouble after that, but I stopped drawing swastikas.

The Germans were good at building motorcycles, and the BMW was one of the best. Pa was a good salesman, and one time he had a preliminary order for 250 BMW motorcycles for the Dutch East Indies Army. When the order was filled for the 250 motorcycles, they were sent to Rotterdam, Holland in preparation to be shipped to Batavia (later renamed Jakarta) and on to Bandung. Unfortunately, the war broke out in Holland in May of 1940. The German army took control of everything in Holland and the 250 motorcycles never got out of the country. Instead, they ended up being used by the German army.

The beginning of the war

With the anxiety and disorder of the world at the time, and knowing the Netherlands had already been invaded by Germany, the Dutch East Indian Army tried to prepare for an expected invasion by the Japanese. My father, along with every other eligible male in the country, was drafted. The army was small and ill-prepared, but if anything, they were confident.

As the war rumors grew, people were told to build bomb shelters. We had a bomb shelter in our back yard, and when the sirens went off, we had to go into the shelter. We would sit there until the sirens blew again to signal the "all clear." One time we were sitting in the bomb shelter and Pa was standing in the doorway. He said, "This war won't last but a couple of months, because everyone knows anything made in Japan isn't of good quality. Our guns and war equipment are far superior to anything they have. Their planes are made out of wax paper and balsa wood, and furthermore, how can they aim their guns and shoot straight with their slanted eyes?!"

Pa went off to get ready for the war. In the beginning, he went to the army during the day and came home to sleep at night. I don't know how long this went on, but it came to a screeching halt when he and all of the other draftees of the Dutch East Indian Army were summoned straightaway by threateningly blasting sirens.

Shortly before the war began, my parents began to build their own house for our family. The new house was large and beautifully designed by an architect. It had huge windows that overlooked the city of Bandung below, and a triple garage, when most houses didn't have even one. It was located outside of the city, farther up in the foothills of the mountain called *Tangkuban Perahu*, which means "upside down boat." The house had just been completed when the war started. In fact, the house was filled with new furniture, beautiful carpets, and linens, and our family was scheduled to move in. Unfortunately, hostilities with the Japanese started several days before the move-in date.

One of the last things my father was to move to the new house was a trunk full of the finest silver and china. As he was on the way up the mountain with this trunk in his Jeep, the air raid sirens went off. He knew he had to report to his base immediately, and he turned around to head back. Knowing he couldn't deliver the trunk, he made a quick stop at the home of an acquaintance to drop it off there, to be picked up later. Unfortunately, later never came. The sirens that day signaled the attack on Bandung, and the battles began, with the Japanese occupation soon to occur. My father was interred in the military POW (Prisoner of War) camp soon after, and, strangely, to the end of his life he never remembered exactly where he left the trunk.

As the war progressed, there were no jobs and most people didn't have money. Bank accounts and businesses were confiscated, and food and other necessities were hard to come by. Most of the men were gone, and women and children had to survive as best they could, so there were many different sorts of barter systems in place. In addition, even in those terrible times, there was always someone ready and able to buy valuable things. My parents always hoped, even though no one in our family ever saw the trunk of precious silver and china again, that its contents may have ensured another needy family's survival through the war, by selling the items.

War

The Battle of Singapore, or the Fall of Singapore, was fought just prior to the invasion of the Dutch East Indies, in February 1942. The city of Singapore, called an "Impregnable Fortress," was an anchor for the operations of the American-British-Dutch-Australian Command (ABDACOM), which was the first Allied joint command of World War II. ABDACOM expected Japan would attack from the sea, and all of their cannons and artillery were trained on the sea. Instead, thousands of paratroopers landed inland. They had wooden bicycles and light tanks they used to easily carry themselves and their weapons through the jungles. Unable to turn their cannons around in time to fight against the paratroopers, and cowering from surprise air attacks as well, Singapore fell in only eight days. Prime Minister Winston Churchill called the Fall of Singapore the worst disaster in British military history. The Japanese began their assault on the Dutch East Indies soon after the Fall of Singapore.

At the beginning of 1942, there was a terrible sea battle between the ABDACOM Allied Forces and the Japanese, called the Battle of the Java Sea. ABDACOM suffered a disastrous defeat by the Imperial Japanese Navy. The fearless commander of the ABDACOM Navy forces, Rear Admiral Karel Doorman, was killed in the battle, and the Dutch Royal Navy surface fleet was basically eradicated from

Asian waters. This was essentially the beginning of the end of Dutch domination of the East Indies and they never again regained control of their colony.

The Battle of the Java Sea ended significant Allied naval operations in South East Asia, and Japanese land forces invaded Java on February 28, 1942. The main ABDACOM naval force had been totally destroyed: 10 ships and more than 2,000 sailors had been lost.

According to Wikipedia®, The Japanese now had control of one of the most important food-producing regions in South East Asia – the island of Java. By conquering the Dutch East Indies, Japan also gained control over the source of the fourth largest oil producer in the world in 1940. The U.S. and British Royal Air Force retreated to Australia. Dutch troops aided by British remnants fought fiercely for a week. In the campaign, the Japanese executed many Allied POWs and sympathizing Indonesians. Despite their logistical problems, the decisive factor in Japan's favor seems to have been air power. Eventually, the Japanese won this decisive battle and ABDACOM forces surrendered on March 9, 1942.

How ironic it was that the Japanese with their "wax paper and balsa wood" planes, would so easily overpower Allied forces in this strategic battle. And how prophetic had been my mother's frightened comment on the day she saw the deep red sky and knew that war was coming.

From the bomb shelter in the back yard of our home, where we fled after an ear-splitting siren told us to go, we heard the surprise bombing of Bandung. The bombing started with the Japanese destroying what was planned to be the Dutch East Indies Air Force's highly-secret fighter planes which had been put together in the middle of the night beneath bamboo shacks at the edge of town. The planes were covered by the shacks along a normal city street that would serve as a runway. Before Allied pilots were able to launch a single plane to counter-attack the Japanese, nearly every one of them was destroyed. Some buildings in downtown Bandung were also destroyed in this attack, including the post office, which was less than a mile from our house.

In the flurry of activity during this surprise attack, someone told my cousin Pieter to run back to the house to close the windows. When he didn't return after a long time, everyone got nervous about what had happened to Pieter, and the bomb shelter door was left open while the adults muttered among themselves.

In utmost fascination, I peeked out the doorway and looked to the sky. Raining down to earth were thousands of sparkling shell casings from the blazing guns of the Japanese fighter planes. Caught in the afternoon sun, they looked like diamonds falling from the sky. Pieter, like me, was mesmerized by the glittering shells and the occasional puffs of black smoke and noisy explosions. He was frozen with his eyes on the sky, just as I was.

After the tragic battle of the Java Sea, and the bombing of our local secret air force, the land battles began. Cities were rapidly conquered after land troops stormed over mountain passes and decimated the pathetically unprepared local army.

I clearly remember standing again with my mother in front of the motorcycle shop on De Groote Postweg, watching in awe as our city of Bandung was overrun with Japanese soldiers. There were hundreds of them – spilling out of Jeeps, trucks, and other military vehicles. They were dusty, dirty, sweaty and tired, but triumphant, after battling and defeating the Allied forces along with the pitifully small and poorly equipped Dutch East Indies Army. We watched in silence as the shock troops (ground soldiers who delivered the first attack) poured into the city.

My head was filled with sounds and especially odors I can hear and smell to this day. Abruptly, in the midst of an endless procession of slowly moving vehicles, a large truck filled with soldiers stopped across the street, in front of our store. Several of the men were pointing at my mother and me, and chattering among themselves. Before I knew what was happening, they got out of their vehicle and motioned repeatedly for me to walk over to them. I was reluctant, but they were insistent and my mother finally nodded that I should go. Under her watchful eye, they began to pat my hair and smile, and it was apparent they were taken with my bright blue eyes. One of the men opened his wallet and showed me a picture of a young boy, who was most likely his son, and he continued to chatter in Japanese and smile and pat me on the head.

Just as suddenly as they stopped, the men loaded onto their truck and drove away. I ran quickly back to my mother. I wasn't afraid. It happened so quickly and was so startling; I didn't have time to be afraid. I guess I was curious most of all. I'm sure my mother had different thoughts.

Registering for POW camps

After the invasion of the shock troops when the Japanese occupation began, everyone in the military had to report or be taken to a POW camp immediately. Everyone else except the natives had to register and state their nationality. People were given a number between one and ten, which determined when they were supposed to report to a civilian prison camp. When their number came up, a summons was sent to their household and those summoned had to take one suitcase and a mattress, and either they walked to the camp, or were taken there. Anyone of partial Dutch or European heritage other than German, and especially anyone who was full-blooded Dutch, English, or American, went to the camps immediately. For example, if you were a full-blooded Dutch person and married to a Dutch or English or American, you were enemy number one, and summoned immediately to the camps. From there it went to higher numbers depending how far removed you were from being full Dutch. It depended on your birth place and your parents.

My mother's mother was native Javanese, and they were considered Asian allies. Her father was German, so my mother might have been given a number nine or ten, which made her unlikely to have to report to a camp. But, she was married to a Dutch man who had been drafted into the Dutch East Indies Army, so she, plus my brother and I got the number seven.

Initially, we felt pretty safe with the number seven, and believed they would leave us alone. Of course, we had no idea of how long the war would last, or how long it would be before our number came up. All we could do was live our lives as best we could, while watching others we knew silently disappear into the ever growing civilian prison camps as time went on.

I tell more later about our living arrangements throughout the war, but the house where we lived the longest during the war was in a new development on a street that wasn't completed. Apparently, the street wasn't on the maps used to assign people to the camps. Our number seven came up at some time during the next three and a half years and we were supposed to report to the civilian camps, but the Japanese couldn't find us to tell us so.

As it happened, a summons for my mother, Huibert and me to report to the camps was finally given to my mother at the beginning of August 1945. We were to report on August 24, which turned out to be only a few days after the atom bomb ended the war. As a result, we never did have to go to the civilian camps.

This speaks about the lack of communication between departments, because we did get mail and had electricity and gas through the war, and we got billed for them. But fortunately for us, the Japanese somehow couldn't find us to deliver our summons to the civilian prison camps until the very end of the war.

Kill all prisoners

There can be no doubt that my life was saved by the atom bomb. I can only imagine the mental agonies suffered by the people who made the decision to drop the bomb and the ones who did the deed. The Atom Bomb was dropped on Hiroshima, Japan on August 6, 1945, and on Nagasaki on August 9, 1945. Yes, there were many lives lost by this extreme reaction, but the lives saved were countless.

Upon their defeat in the war after the bombings, a fire was set at Japanese Imperial Army headquarters in Taiwan to deliberately destroy evidence that might incriminate them. Some documents survived the fire and they have remained classified until the year 2000, when some documents were declassified and made public. Two of the surviving documents pertain directly to Philippine and Dutch East Indies detainees.

One document, No. 2697, certified as Exhibit J in Doc. No. 2687, is the **order telling guards to flee to avoid prosecution for war crimes.** This order was made on August 20, 1945, five days after the surrender, and was made because of severe mistreatment of POWs and civilian prisoners, despite the 1929 Geneva Convention agreement. The Japanese knew they would be punished for their severe and inhumane treatment of prisoners, and they were taking this cowardly way out of being held responsible for their despicable treatment of prisoners.

The second document, No. 2701 (Certified as Exhibit "O" in Doc. No. 2687) is bone-chilling in its blunt wording about **"final disposition" of all prisoners**. This Kill All Prisoners decree was made on August 8, 1944, a full year before the atom bomb was deployed. The document was posted and seen by POWs throughout the Philippines, Dutch East Indies, and other Asian POW and civilian camps.

The original order is now in the U.S. National Archives in Washington, D.C. A partial English translation states:

> Under the present situation if there were a mere explosion or fire, a shelter for the time being could be had in nearby buildings such as the school, a warehouse, or the like. However, at such time as the situation became urgent and it be extremely important, the POWs will be concentrated and confined in their present location, and under heavy guard the preparation for the final disposition will be made.

The time and method of this disposition are as follows:

1. The time

   Although the basic aim is to act under superior orders, individual disposition may be made in the following circumstances:

   a) When an uprising of large numbers cannot be suppressed without the use of firearms.

   b) When escapees from the camp may turn into a hostile fighting force.

2. The Method

   a) **Whether they (prisoners) are destroyed individually or in groups, or however it is done, with mass bombing, poisonous smoke, poisons, drowning, decapitations, or what, dispose of them as the situation dictates.**

   b) **In any case it is the aim not to allow the escape of a single one, to annihilate them all, and not to leave any traces.**

The original Kill All Order appears on the following page, and was provided by Wes Injerd, of Hillsboro, Oregon. Injerd has continued the extensive work of Roger Mansell who was the founder of the Center for Research, Allied POWs Under the Japanese.

One of the ironies of this incredibly horrible official order relates to "The time." By the time this order was posted in 1944, prisoners were so emaciated and deliberately weakened by starvation and overwork, there was no possible way for them to form any sort of uprising or hostile fighting force.

It has been determined that the "superior orders" referred to in the document meant that if prisoners did not form an uprising themselves, thereby causing their immediate murders, the routine killing of all POWs and civilian internees was to start in September 1945.

"The Method" in its blunt and passionless verbiage for "final disposition," speaks for itself.

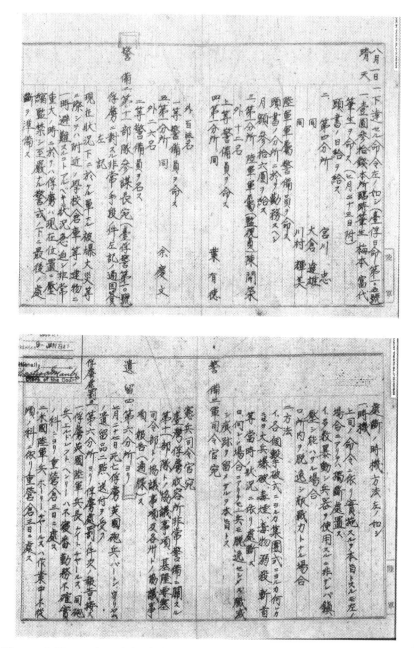

Figure 9 Pages 1 and 2 of the original Kill All Prisoners order, written in Japanese. These were posted in POW camps in 1944. The original document is in the U.S. National Archives in Washington, D.C. Provided by Wes Injerd; documents in public domain.

POW camps

Because my father was military, he was forced to enter the POW camp immediately after the Japanese occupation. The only POW camp of which I was aware at the beginning of the war was created out of what had been the Dutch East Indies Army military base in Bandung. The Japanese put barbed wire all around the camp and posted sentries and that was it. People were able to just walk by it or across the street, and you could see the prisoners living there. It was in the city and not all that far from where we lived.

Before long, there were hundreds of POW and civilian prison camps throughout the Dutch East Indies, and internees were moved between them. In fact, many prisoners were moved between islands by Japanese troop transport ships. This endangered prisoners to the possibility of being torpedoed by Allied submarines because the ships were believed to be carrying enemy troops. More is told about "Japanese hell ships" farther in this chapter.

It is not possible to quote the number of civilian and military prisoners of war in the Dutch East Indies. Every source investigated gives widely disparate numbers. However, it is not the intent of this document to verify numbers. The intent instead, is to share my own observations, memories, and knowledge of how life endured during a frightening, cruelly heartless time when man's inhumanity to man threatened to destroy the world, and did destroy ours.

What is known from prisoners who escaped or were released at the end of the war is that prisoners, including women and children, routinely suffered savage beatings from Japanese soldiers. Their heads were shaved and they were forced to stand for hours in the blazing sun. They were regularly ordered to parade, bowing in the direction of Japan. If they didn't bow properly, they were beaten. Food was withheld and what little food was provided was watered down and often filled with maggots and weevils, or visibly rotten. Internees were deliberately starved, while being expected to work many hours at various jobs, either backbreaking hard labor or disgusting work like cleaning overflowing latrines.

Some camps were worse than others, usually depending on the camp's commander. One commander, Captain Kenichi Sonei from Tjideng internment camp in Batavia (now Jakarta), was called a "cruel lunatic," by survivors. He forced prisoners in the severely overcrowded prison to constantly march day and night so everyone could be accounted for. After the war, Sonei was executed for his crimes.

Robert L. Hudson met Manny Lawton a number of years ago at a POW gathering. Lawton, a Death March survivor and ex-POW has since passed away, but Hudson uses on his web page Lawton's "Definition of Hell." Lawton said, "Hell is not a place it's a condition." Knowing what I've learned through research for this book, I know it is both and Hell surely exists on this earth in the form of war.

In the beginning of the Japanese occupation, my father had permission to run his business for a few days and he stayed at home at night. However, the time came quite soon when the Japanese confiscated everything connected to the business and Pa left home to stay at the camp. He was dressed in a military uniform when he left that day with his suitcase, and my mother filled his canteen or flask with warm tea for him to take along.

I did see Pa one time while he was in the Bandung POW camp. I don't know how this came about, but I went to the camp with one of our native servants, who were called *babus*. I know it was too far to walk, and we might have gone by bicycle or *dokar*.

When we got there, I was told to walk across the street. All at once, I saw my father behind the wire. He was pointing to the gate of the camp. There was a Japanese guard there, but I, as a young child, was allowed to go into the camp and be greeted and hugged by my father. I learned later that no adult would have been allowed to enter the camp and leave again. I stood there feeling so happy to have Pa kneeling in front of me and hugging me. After a few minutes I walked out of the gate and that was the last time I saw my father until the end of the war, almost four years later.

Frits van Demmeltraadt's POW experience

As I said earlier, we had no knowledge of where my father was imprisoned and other than that first short sighting for me, we didn't see or hear from him for almost four years. We learned later he was kept in the POW camp in Bandung for a short time at the beginning of the war. He was then moved to a neighboring town called Tjimahi (current spelling Cimahi) where large numbers of civilians and POWs were held. I have learned very recently Pa then was taken to Malaya POW Camp #1, namely the Changi prison, in Singapore. At least 10,000 prisoners came and went from Changi as they were transferred to other camps for specific work projects. As many as 4,000 at a time stayed there in a prison built for 800.

My father eventually was sent to Pakanbaru (new spelling) a city in Sumatra where prisoners were forced to build a railway amid horrifying conditions of neglect and torture.

Wikipedia® describes Pakanbaru this way:

> During the Second World War from February 1942 to August 1945 the city of Pakanbaru was occupied by the armed forces of Japan. In an effort to strengthen the military and logistical infrastructure in this part of Sumatra, the Japanese launched the construction of a 215 km long railway, connecting Pakanbaru to the coast of Malacca Straits.
>
> The Pakanbaru Railway was constructed under harsh conditions by forced labor. 6,500 Dutch, mostly Indo-Europeans, and British prisoners of war and over 100,000 Indonesians, mostly Javanese, forced-workers called *Romusha* were put to work by the Japanese army. By the time the work was completed in August 1945 almost a third of the European POWs and over half of the Indonesian coolies had died. The railway was never fully utilized. Today it remains unused and in an advanced state of decay.

The small piece inserted below is from an article by George Duffy and Australian Dr. van Ramshorst, from the website by John Winterbotham.[4] Duffy and van Ramshorst were also prisoners at Pakanbaru, and they state, "A Dutch author dubbed Pakanbaru 'The Death Railway through the Jungle.'"

The website quotes Duffy and van Ramshorst freely and their description is indicative of the type of conditions prisoners endured at this harsh and merciless camp.

> The exhausted POWs, who were forced, during the Japanese occupation, to construct a railway line 215 kilometers long right through the mid-Sumatran tropical jungle, had no escape. For over a year, from late May 1944 until Japanese capitulation on 15 August 1945, they were subject to the whims of their cruel Korean guards and to their Japanese masters, who had been ordered by Tokyo to construct a railway line between Pakanbaru and Muara at the cost of so many human lives. They acquitted themselves very well in this task. More than 10,000 native slave laborers and nearly 700 whites, mostly Dutch POWs died in the torrid Sumatran jungle of malnutrition, beriberi, tropical sores, malaria and dysentery. And this does not include the 1,626 victims who perished on the way to Sumatra, torpedoed by the Allies on board the POW ships "Van Waerwijck" and "Junyo Mary."
>
> Indeed, death was no stranger there. We were overworked, underfed, provided with little medicine, and subjected to constant physical and mental abuse by our Japanese overseers. A hospital existed in name only. It was simply a dilapidated bamboo-framed, thatched roof barracks where the sick were placed to await their eventual death. Once in a while a man recovered his health and returned to the daily camp routine, but it was not the rule.

---

[4] Permission received August 12, 2014 to use information from the webpage www.australian-pow-ww2.com/sumatra_17.html

All the suffering in this case was for nothing. The railway line no longer exists. Kilometers of rail have been looted or sold as scrap iron. And what remains is slowly rusting away in the stagnant black marsh water of the impenetrable Sumatran Jungle.

My father was a mechanic and worked on the trucks and automobile engines used for the railway at Pakanbaru. He developed malaria there, from which he struggled for the rest of his life. However, his daily life and treatment in this camp as well as the others where he was held captive remains a mystery to our family because he never talked about it.

Unfortunately, others have been reluctant to talk about their experiences in World War II as well, and the horrors experienced by prisoners have gone undocumented for too long. With the advent of the Internet, more and more information is being collected and survivors and their families are finally recording what happened so long ago.

The one incident my father did tell about his captivity speaks of his amazing sense of humor and the positive attitude he maintained his whole life. It is also an example of the type of sadistic treatment given to prisoners during their captivity at Pakanbaru.

Pa told of a guard coming to their barracks one day, which happened to be Easter morning. Prisoners didn't have to work that day and all were in their barracks. The guard said Pa and one other man were summoned to see the camp commander, and they were marched off to his office. They were made to stand at attention outside for an hour or so, and were fearful during this time because everyone knew being summoned there was always a bad sign. After an hour passed, the guard came back and told the two men to kneel on the ground. While kneeling there for another hour at least, the commander came out and walked toward them. As he approached them, he drew his pistol, causing Pa and his friend to flinch and prepare to be shot. Instead of shooting, the commander looked harshly at them, and then "pistol whipped" each of the men hard on the face with his gun, turned, and walked away. The guard told the men to stand up and go back to their barracks, which they did post haste.

As my father told the story later, he said when he got back to the barracks he had a huge lump on the side of his face, like an egg. He laughed and said he didn't know why they were summoned to the commander that day, but he had found his Easter egg that year after all.

Another railway

The Indonesians had no trust for the Japanese, even though the natives were not put in the prison camps as were the Europeans and Indos during the war. One reason is the Japanese cruelly used native Indonesian natives along with European POWs to build such projects as the Pakanbaru Railway described above, and the Burma Railway.[5] I know the Dutch and other Europeans suffered when they were forced to do this work, and I heard for every railroad tie

---

[5] From Wikipedia®: The Burma Railway, also known as "the Death Railway," was a 415 kilometer (258 mile) railway between Bangkok, Thailand, and Rangoon, Burma (now Yangon, Myanmar), built by the Empire of Japan in 1943, to support its forces in the Burma campaign of World War II. The line was closed in 1947, but the section between Nong Pla Duk and Nam Tok was reopened ten years later in 1957. Forced labor was used in its construction. About 180,000 Asian laborers and 60,000 Allied prisoners of war worked on the railway. Of these, around 90,000 Asian laborers (mainly *Romusha*) and 12,399 Allied POWs died as a direct result of the project. The dead POWs included 6,318 British personnel, 2,815 Australians, 2,490 Dutch, about 356 Americans and a smaller number of Canadians and New Zealanders. The U.S. Library of Congress estimates that in Java, between four to 10 million *Romusha* were forced to work by the Japanese military.

The Japanese military made extensive use of such forced labor during the construction of the Burma-Thailand Railway during 1942-43 and the Pakanbaru Railway on Sumatra in 1943-45. The death rate among *Romusha*, from atrocities, starvation-diet, and disease far outstripped the death rate among Allied prisoners of war. About half the forced laborers engaged on the railroad construction died.

they laid, two or three men died. The Indonesians suffered, too, and while they were eventually "liberated" by the Japanese, there was much bitterness between them because of cruelties by the Japanese to the Indonesians.

Japanese hell ships

From Wikipedia®: In May 1942, the Japanese began transferring POWs by sea. Similar to treatment on the Bataan Death March, prisoners were often crammed into cargo holds with little air, food or water for journeys that would last for many days. Many died due to asphyxia, starvation or dysentery. Some POWs became delirious and unresponsive in their environment of heat, humidity, and lack of oxygen, food, and water. These unmarked prisoner transports, called Japanese hell ships, were targeted as enemy ships by Allied submarines and aircraft. More than 20,000 Allied POWs died at sea when the transport ships carrying them were attacked by Allied submarines and aircraft.

My grandmother van Demmeltraadt had a relative who was called Oom Jamie (all male relatives and even some good friends were called "Uncle" or "Oom"). Jamie was drafted in the Dutch East Indies Army and eventually imprisoned by the Japanese as a POW. He was with a group of other POWs who were sent to another prison in Burma on one of the Japanese hell ships. As described above, the American troops torpedoed some of these ships, and Oom Jamie's ship was one that was attacked. However, Jamie was one of the fortunate prisoners who survived the attack and lived to tell the story.

As Huibert remembers hearing it, when the ship was torpedoed, somehow Jamie was able to scramble his way to the upper deck from the hold below. Most of the Japanese soldiers were desperate to save their own skins and were fleeing the ship. Jamie saw one of the Japanese soldiers, a Korean guard who had been conscripted by the

Japanese and known to be one of the meanest of his captors, coming his way. Jamie was frantic to get away and he grabbed a heavy tool nearby and hit the guard hard over the head. The guard fell into the hold which was filling with water, and as Jamie dived over the rail to the ocean below, he presumed that the guard was dead.

Weakened, exhausted, and half-drowned, survivors of the wreck were plucked from the sea by Japanese lifeboats and eventually taken to an island. Amid the chaos there, Jamie saw the Korean guard with a bandage on his head and he knew he was searching for his attacker, as the man was watchfully checking out every prisoner who had been rescued. Surprised to see the man had survived, after first thinking he was seeing a ghost, Jamie went to his own lieutenant and told him what had happened. The lieutenant thought quickly and told Jamie to lie on a stretcher and they wrapped him in bandages as though he were heavily wounded. Two other prisoners carried the stretcher past the Korean guard without detection.

Jamie was sent to another prison camp and he did survive the war. In fact, before we went to Holland after the war, we saw Jamie in Jakarta during the *Bersiap* period (see Chapter 3, The Bersiap). He was still in the Dutch East Indies Army in a special division called *Gajah Merah*, known to be especially fierce fighters. This group eventually cleaned up the rebels on the island of Bali during the *Bersiap*. We don't know what happened to Oom Jamie or any of his family after that event.

Living through the war

All of the Dutch schools were closed at the beginning of the war in February 1942. It was too dangerous for children to be in the school buildings because at any moment there could be an air raid. I was in first grade at the time and didn't resume my schooling until we went to Holland after the war.

The Japanese seized possession of many houses during the war, but they didn't plunder. They didn't destroy property or steal goods. However, once the Japanese defeated the Dutch army, the regular police were not operating, and groups of Indonesians began to do some looting in areas where the Japanese had not yet established law and order. When the Japanese found out about the stealing, they would find someone who knew who did it, and they had their own way of dealing with the perpetrators. They would interrogate the thieves as to which arm they used to carry items, and chop off that hand. They also dragged some looters behind a car around the city square. Word got around and the looting soon stopped.

Before my father disappeared to the camps, we lived behind the motorcycle store. Living there at that time were my parents, Huibert and me, plus my father's brother, Oom Joop, and his wife and three kids. Maktje, my grandmother's sister and my nursemaid, always lived with us too, but she died shortly before the real hostilities began.

At the time Maktje died, death was unknown to me and I didn't fully understand she wasn't coming back. I kept waiting for her to join me in the big bed we shared in the room where Huibert also slept. The hole she left in our lives was soon filled with new adventures, many of them fearsome, and all of them altered from what had truly been paradise to our family.

Many moves

Oom Joop went to the camps about a year after my father did; perhaps because he was non-military he didn't have to go right away. Huibert reminds me that during the war Oom Joop's family left our house and went to live with a woman who was a medium. People often came to her with questions, and she would lay out her cards and read the future, sometimes with a dark and foreboding look in her eye. I was never comfortable in her house. It was dark and gloomy and there was always an unpleasant smell of burning incense which made it frightening. After Oom Joop went into the camp, his wife, Tante Cor, and her three children moved again and we didn't have much contact with them for the rest of the war. I never again went to the house of the medium.

Sadly, none of our family ever lived in the beautiful new house. With my father gone to the camps, the move-in date was cancelled. As the war went on and things got worse and worse, my mother had to sell or trade some of the furnishings in the house for necessities for our family. How she got access to them, I'll never know, because there were no cars or gas or manpower to move anything, and it was far up the mountain from Bandung. Remarkably, the Japanese never confiscated the house. It was a long distance out of town and sort of hidden behind trees and rocks and such, so they may not have been able to find it. After the war it was lost to us, and we heard the house eventually became a school for the area.

Soon after my father went to the POW camp, my mother had a terrible asthma attack, and had to be hospitalized. She must have arranged for Huibert and me to go to live with her good friend, Sjaan Brund. Sjaan was a very dark Ambonese woman with a Christian heart of gold, but she had no children. She was married to a tall blond full Dutch man, and she spoke perfect Dutch. We always said that Sjaan was more Dutch than the real Dutch because of the way she spoke, her manners, and the way she kept her house. For example, at 11 o'clock it was coffee time and you got your coffee and one small cookie. The rule was you were supposed to decline the offer of a second cookie, if it should come. One cookie was enough and that was how it was.

Before long, Tante Sjaan's husband, Oom Ko, was summoned to go to the camps. I watched him go off in a *dokar* with his one suitcase and his mattress all rolled up. He smiled when he left, but it was a sad smile, and I knew his smile wouldn't last long.

We lived with Tante Sjaan for only about a month. After my mother left the hospital, she went to a sort of nursing home for a while and I went to visit her there. This is a frightening memory for me because I couldn't understand why she didn't come home. It was terrible for me to leave her there, and is one of my worst childhood memories.

After my mother finally came back we had a good reunion. We

moved then to what was considered an area of the economic lower class. The neighborhood was called Tuindorp, and Huibert and I loved it there because we could roam around all day barefoot, and play all the time because there was no school. We lived in Tuindorp with Tante Marie, my mother's older sister, and their brother, Oom Ben, who had been with the police department and was single.

This was where I met my friend Bonthy Kiliaan who also had moved to this neighborhood with his family, including his beautiful sister. They came to live with his aunt, and one day there he was. We became friends right away and Bonthy and I have forever remained good friends. Bonthy is one year older than I, and when we first met I was immediately impressed with his stature. He stood tall and straight and has maintained that upright posture life-long. His sister was knock-out gorgeous and even though she was several years older than any of us, I think all the boys were in love with her.

After a year or so we moved uptown Bandung to Ring Boulevaard, a newly developed area of the city, to the house of a woman who was the wife of a colonel in the Dutch Army. Mr. and Mrs. Allirol were Dutch, except that she might have been part German or Swiss because she didn't have to go to the camps. They were well to do and she had amazing furniture and a large and spread-out house. There were big chests lined with camphor, and other beautiful pieces of furniture. We stayed in this house for the longest time during the war.

It was common to have one building for the family, and another sort of apartment attached to it for guests. The apartment had all facilities so someone living there didn't have to have contact at all with the people in the main house. Mrs. Allirol lived in the apartment they called the pavilion. She was alone with her two dachshunds, and the rest of us lived in the larger part of the house.

There was also another woman who lived there, Mrs. Tegelaar, and her 12 year-old son. She was an Indo woman who was also part Japanese, and Oom Ben knew her from when he was a captain for the police. She and her son lived in one room of the big house. Mrs. Tegelaar had tuberculosis and had been in a sanatorium at one time.

I always knew TB was infectious, but I thought no one in our family had been affected by Mrs. Tegelaar's condition. I found out recently, now that my brother is more than 80 years old, Huibert did in fact contract a latent form of the disease when he was a child. He said he had "one lesion," but it healed successfully and never led to full-blown tuberculosis.

My bear

The people left behind when their loved ones went to the camps had to scramble to live. There were few jobs, bank accounts had been seized, and daily living was difficult at best. One way people survived was to sell their possessions. Inevitably, some people still had money in spite of the horrors of war. In our culture, I know it was primarily the Chinese who had money. How they got it, I'll never know, but they were the ones to buy when others had to sell. I suspect my mother sold to the Chinese whatever she could take out of the new house.

There came a time when my mother approached me with a shocking request. She wanted to sell my bear! This was the huge teddy bear that I had gotten from Santa Claus, and my most prized and loved companion. That bear was part of me! My mother said there was no longer any money in the house and we needed to eat. Somehow she found a family who was interested in buying the bear for their children, and she grabbed the opportunity and sold the bear.

Figure 10 Onno and Bear.
Photo taken by Erna van Demmeltraadt, deceased

This was an indescribable catastrophe for me, and as I look back now, it must have been horrible for my mother to have to do this. She knew how much I loved Bear and what he meant to me, but she was responsible for feeding a houseful of people, and she most likely saw no other choice.

My light brown bear had a lighter tan, friendly face. He was stuffed with straw, and had a sort of mesh skin that was covered with long hair, probably made of wool. I had always been careful with Bear to not get him dirty and he always smelled good. Even after cuddling with Bear for more than three years, he still looked new. It was heartbreaking for me to part with my best friend, but I knew I had to do it. I remember the moment to this day when I handed the bear to my mother to take him away, and how I suffered with his loss.

When the war was finally over, my mother came to me and asked if I wanted the bear back. Apparently the people who bought the bear had to leave the country in a hurry, which wasn't unusual after the war, and they must have told my mother she could have it back.

Even two years later I could hardly wait to hold Bear in my arms again. Sadly, he arrived in pieces. One arm was missing, one leg was hanging, and patches of his hair were gone. I couldn't imagine how those children had abused my bear, but there he was and I loved him all the same. I didn't play with the bear anymore because I was older then, but he sat at the end of my bed and he was just there for me. Later, my mother said she had found someone who could repair the bear, and soon he was taken to get repaired.

I grew older and of course found other interests in motorcycles and school and all, but Bear still sat on my bed. Before I knew it, I went to Holland to go to college when I was 17. My mother came three years later to live in Holland and I'll be darned if she didn't bring that bear all the way from Indonesia to Holland when I was going to college. She kept the bear with her through the years. After my mother died, and I was married and living in America, my Tante Marie wrote to ask if I wanted her to send the bear! By that time, the poor bear had endured years of storage in the humidity of Holland

and I'm sure he didn't have much hair or anything else left, so I told
her to just throw him away. What a sad end to my faithful friend.

Fertile land

The city of Bandung had been built on land that had at one
time been a huge lake at the foot of volcanoes all around it. All of
the volcanoes are still there and they still spit smoke on occasion,
but these particular volcanoes haven't erupted for at least the last
hundred years that I know of. The most northern and most well-
known volcano is *Tangkuban Perahu* which can still be seen from
anywhere in the city. It was a sort of "compass" to us. We always
knew which direction was north, because that's where we could see
Tangkuban Perahu.

The story is at some time in the far distant past, there was a split
in the earth, most likely from a huge earthquake, which caused all
of the water in the huge lake to run away to the northwest toward
Jakarta, a distance of about 100 miles. This left a huge "bowl" with
fertile land where the city of Bandung grew. I've always said that the
land around Bandung is so fertile if you put a broom handle in the
ground, it would grow brooms.

Daily Survival

During the Japanese occupation, the city of Bandung was divided
into areas, similar to precincts here in Minnesota. Food was scarce
because the Japanese confiscated most of it for their troops, and a
minimal amount went to the camps for the prisoners. Of course, there
were natural fruits and vegetables available and the markets continued
to be held. However, the major problem was transportation. There
was no gas and there were no vehicles to use to get to the markets
because most of those items were confiscated by the Japanese also.
Instead, there was a program where people got a certain amount of
rice using an identification card.

Each precinct had a leader appointed by the Japanese, who was responsible to get the right amount of rice to a distribution point where the people picked it up. The position of precinct leader was popular because that person usually got first choice on things given away and extra foods as well.

Huibert and I, plus some other boys in the neighborhood were always looking for something to do and a way to make a little money. Somehow we acquired an old baby buggy we converted into a little cart. We used the cart to haul rice for various neighbors when the precinct leader brought it back to the distribution point. We made a few pennies a week by doing this.

When we were living on Ring Boulevaard at the home of Mrs. Allirol, one day we were summoned to the neighborhood leader. He said the Japanese had decided each household should have some sort of garden to raise vegetables, and we could use a certain small area to plant one. Close to the neighborhood square was a buildable lot which had not been sold so it was open to use for these small gardens. I was responsible for disbursing seeds to people in the neighborhood for them to plant.

Huibert and I worked on our little garden of cucumbers, tomatoes, green beans, and pea pods, and watered it faithfully from the open sewer running behind every house. There were small canals about a foot and a half wide behind the houses. Each house had a pipe running from it to the little canal, and all of the wastewater went into this canal. Eventually the water went to the river, the Cikapundung, and the river went all the way to the sea.

We used a little bucket to get wastewater from the canal to water the plants, and with the fertile soil and natural fertilizer in the water, they grew like crazy. In the end, they mostly tasted good; the beans were tender and crisp, the cucumbers were crunchy and delicious, and the tomatoes looked wonderful. I could hardly wait to taste one. I finally took a big bite of a juicy red tomato, expecting it to be really great, and instead it tasted like shit. I mean literally, like shit. For some reason, only the tomatoes picked up the nasty taste and scent of the excrement which floated along in the water we used to feed our plants.

In my later life when I grew tomatoes, I found they always seem to pull out the taste and scent of the ground they are grown in. Other plants may filter the water in some way, but the tomato seems to suck it all up without filtering. I learned the hard way a tomato is one plant that is only as sweet as the ground and fertilizer you give it.

By order of the Japanese we all had to grow a certain plant, called the *djarak*. It was a plant about five or six feet high with small, round, green fruits which were not edible, but they were extremely high in oil content. (I've recently learned castor oil is made from this plant.) Everyone had to have it planted in their yards, but nobody ever seemed to harvest it. The Japanese planned to make lubricant oil from it for their war machines, but nobody ever came to get it and the plants just rotted on the vine. I know some people sabotaged the effort and didn't water their plants so they wouldn't grow, but it never really mattered, because the fruits were never collected.

Having the garden was a good thing because it provided food we all needed. Meat was only available through barter or cash, so we hardly ate any meat at all throughout the war. For protein, we had tofu and tempe and some beans, but never meat. Tofu and tempe are both made from soy beans; it's the process of making them that's different. I think tempe is fermented. Both tempe and tofu have been staples of the Asian diet as long as I can remember.

The gardening project also provided entertainment at a time when there wasn't much else to do. When Huibert and I were finished with our gardening chores, we'd look around for other boys working on their gardens and we ended up playing in the clods of dirt or throwing clay at each other, having fun in some way.

Another regulation the Japanese instigated was for each neighborhood to have a night patrol. It was manned by someone from each household in the neighborhood who took turns, or they could have a representative do it for them. I got to do it, young as I was. I was about eight then, and I went out with my Oom Ben

Schmidt, the former policeman. We started about 10 o'clock in the evening and patrolled the street by walking around to be sure there were no break-ins or trouble happening. We never really encountered any trouble, but we probably made so much noise walking around, anyone with ill intent had plenty of time to hide.

All through the war, there was a procedure in place where if anyone was stopped while riding in a vehicle or bicycle or anything with wheels, they had to stop, get out of the vehicle, stand next to it, and bow to the soldier. This was required because every soldier was a representative of the Japanese Emperor and everyone had to bow in respect.

The son of the lady who had TB was older than I and a lot taller and every time something was needed, he would get on his bicycle and go into town. I tagged along with him whenever I could, and on one of our trips when we came back from the town, we were stopped at the entrance to our street by a Japanese soldier. We bowed to him, but he was growling and shouting at us in his poor Indonesian, and we tried to make him understand we lived there. He finally let us go around the corner and into our street, although we had to walk our bikes because he wouldn't let us ride. Of course, we left only after we deeply bowed to him again.

The Japanese mandated every household to designate a representative to do morning calisthenics. Only one member of the family had to go to the assembly place, but there had to be one person from each household. I liked doing this, so I became the designated representative from our house. Other boys from the neighborhood were there, too, and it was a lot of fun. We had to stand in line early in the morning, and "fall in" like we were going to march or something. One guy in front led the exercises and we had to follow him and do whatever he did. He counted in Japanese as we did toe touches, knee bends, squats, and all sorts of exercises. Ichy-ni (one-two) san-shi (three-four) go-ruku (five-six) shichi-hachi (seven-eight) ku-ju (nine-ten).

It was pretty serious, but the boys in the neighborhood had fun doing it. There were no women or girls there; it was just boys and men. The calisthenics started about six o'clock and lasted about 20 minutes every day.

With no school during the war, we played all the time. There were several rivers in the city. The water came from the mountains mainly, and of course all of the canals with the sewer water went into the rivers, too. My friend Bonthy and I learned to swim in the river and we always had a lot of fun there. The current was pretty fast, and somehow the water cleansed itself to a certain degree. Sometimes a floating human "torpedo" would go flying by when we were playing in the water, but we just pushed it aside and kept on playing.

Soldiers on our street

Ring Boulevaard was on the eastern edge of town and was part of a new development begun shortly before the war. Only three houses were inhabited on our street which was about a mile long, and two other houses were empty. Across the street from our house was a little ravine that had been designated to become a city park. There was a stream at the bottom of the ravine with cold fresh water coming from high in the mountains.

The street that ran by the ravine, which went by our house too, was never finished. The street was gravel, steam-rolled and topped with larger gravel, pretty big rocks actually, in preparation for the blacktop which was started, but never finished. Because we always went barefoot as kids, it was really tough to walk on the gravel, and in the afternoon when the sun was hottest, it was awful – those rocks were hot! I ran to the blacktop thinking it would be easier to walk on, and it was even hotter! We always kept to the side of the street where the sand was softer and it was easier to walk.

One day Huibert and I were walking down our street and saw some busy activity at the ravine. Many people were freely walking around with little carts carrying gardening supplies. It soon became clear that the extremely fertile ravine was being planted and cared for by prisoners from the camp. Of course, the prisoners weren't free at all, as there were many Japanese guards watching them closely while they worked.

When we got home, there were many questions about what we had seen and what was happening. Thereafter, the prisoners were marched to our street every day and they worked with planting the ground. In the afternoons, the prisoners were gathered in formation to make sure all of them were there. They counted off in rows three or four deep, and the guard in front was responsible to know they were returning to the camp with everyone accounted for, and off they marched.

Soldiers in our home

The Japanese required us to keep our windows covered. We had to tape newspapers over them so no light seeped out at night, which could possibly enable the evil Americans to find the town. Also, there were fake air raids for training purposes, and there was no notice of whether an air raid was real or fake. During the fake air raids, there would be surprise inspections by Japanese officers to see if there might be light leaking.

We dutifully covered all of our windows, but to help us know who might be at our door, we had a tiny corner of the paper that could be lifted. Sure enough, one night there was a knock on our door, and outside were two strange men. Tante Marie answered the door to a smiling man in sunglasses, who was obviously a Japanese soldier, but pretending to be an Indonesian. He politely asked her if she could possibly smuggle a little note to a prisoner in the camps. Tante Marie immediately saw through this silly deception, and she was not intimidated in the least as some might have been. Tante Marie started yelling at the man saying, "What are you asking me to do?! This is not right! I won't do anything of the kind. In fact, I'm going to report you to the *Kempeitai!*"

The *Kempeitai* was the highest secret Japanese military police force – as bad as or worse than the Gestapo in Germany or the

KGB in Russia – which was much feared by everyone, including the Japanese soldiers. The word was if anyone ever got into the hands of the *Kempeitai*, they never came out whole; guilty or not, they were damaged.

Tante Marie was not backing down, and she kept threatening to call the *Kempeitai* and yelled at the man until he gave her a shocked look and finally turned and left, never to be seen again.

This was our first encounter with the Japanese in our home, and it was pretty scary. I'll never forget Tante Marie's gutsy reaction, but apparently she passed the test and we didn't have that sort of invasion again.

We did have an encounter with the real *Kempeitai* in our home one time, however. There was a man who was like a town crier who rode around on his bicycle in the neighborhoods and shouted "Alarm, alarm!" in Japanese. This meant there could possibly be an air raid or something. We had to turn off all the lights and be sure no light leaked out of the house, until another crier would come around later with the all clear. One evening in the middle of the war, we were quietly sitting in our living room, and it was pitch dark outside. We didn't hear any call of alarm or anything and all was quiet. We learned later there was one small window open in the back of the house, of which we weren't aware.

Suddenly we heard shouting and heavy footsteps on our porch and the door was forcefully opened with no knocking or anything. Tante Marie was immediately faced with a huge angry officer with a band on his arm that identified him as being from the *Kempeitai*. He kept on shouting and shouting and was dreadfully menacing. We couldn't understand what he was shouting, but there was another man with him who said it had been reported there was light coming from our house.

The shouting officer said everyone had to be arrested and was ready to haul us all off. Tante Marie tried to reason with him and told him there were children there who needed to be cared for, and then she told him about the woman who had TB. He immediately moved away and didn't want to have anything to do with the sick woman. He agreed someone had to take care of the children, so he went marching off to the other part of the house where Mrs. Allirol was living alone, and he started screaming at her.

Mrs. Allirol was a starched and formal lady who dressed up for tea time every day. Sometimes she had other ladies in for tea, but every day she dressed in elegant clothes and high heels. I went to the side of the house and I saw the shouting officer dragging Mrs. Allirol with her beautiful evening shoes trailing in the dirt, trying to resist and begging for mercy. He dragged her by her arms to his car, with her crying and screaming all the way.

In the meantime, Oom Ben had already gone to bed and all of the shouting woke him up. He came into the room and the *Kempeitai* officer almost went berserk. After much more shouting and arm waving, they hauled both Oom Ben and Mrs. Allirol to their car and drove away.

By this time it was about nine o'clock and it got extremely quiet after they left. We were all afraid we'd never see either of them again. In fact, the shock of seeing both of them dragged brutally away has never left my mind and I can still hear Mrs. Allirol's dreadful cries.[6]

Oom Ben and Mrs. Allirol were taken to *Kempeitai* headquarters and interrogated. Oom Ben was accused of being an American spy who was trying to escape through the open window. No matter how he tried to explain he was just asleep, they said he was lying and started to beat him up. Oom Ben told us later the man who was hitting him picked up a ruler and hit him in the face with it. He then aimed for his ear, and Oom Ben turned his head and the ruler hit him in the back of his head on his skull and broke the ruler. A piece of the ruler flew in the direction of a sergeant who was sitting at a

[6] In recent years I've learned about horrible acts perpetrated on Dutch women in Indonesia during the war. One story is told in the book *Fifty Years of Silence*, by Jan Ruff-O'Hearne, an internee in a Java camp, who was raped day and night for months by Japanese soldiers. This could have been the fate of any of the women we knew.

desk doing his paperwork, and hit him in his arm. The sergeant then started shouting and swearing at the interrogator and that was the end of the beating.

Oom Ben was marched outside and made to stand at attention for the rest of the night. There were several other people arrested that evening for the same sort of thing. They were all forced to stand at attention all night, including Mrs. Allirol, who most likely had some whacks given to her also. That was just the way they operated – even if someone wasn't guilty of anything, they still got hit so many times.

At some time during the night, Mrs. Allirol said she had to go to the bathroom. There was some giggling and the men told her to just go in her pants like they did. She couldn't do that, so the prisoners moved slowly together and stood in front of her so she could pee on the ground outside the sight of the *Kempeitai* men. At least a fragment of her dignity might have been saved by their actions.

The next day, about noon or so, both Mrs. Allirol and Oom Ben came home in a *dokar*. The terrible smell of them as they got out of the *dokar* and went into the house has never left my mind. There was the smell of fear, of blood, of terror, and more. This was a horrendous experience for them, and we were much relieved to see them come home. I can only guess at their mental anguish, but at least their bodies were whole.

A friendly face from the enemy

After the prisoners had been working in the ravine for a couple of weeks, another Japanese soldier came to our door. This time he didn't knock. He opened the door quickly and immediately strutted in with his huge rifle and its frightening bayonet that was carried on his side like a sword. Brave and fearless, Tante Marie rushed to the door and the man pointed at the large couch in our living room and indicated he wanted to take a nap. Tante Marie was to wake him in a half hour so he could go back to guard duty. And by the way, if any other Japanese soldier should come, he should be woken up immediately.

Straightaway, he lay on his back on the couch with his rifle between his legs and his cap over his eyes, and began to snore. In a half hour, Tante Marie woke him and he went on his way. The next day he came back and did the same thing, and this time he told Tante Marie his name, which was Jastak.

Jastak was a Korean who had been conscripted by the Japanese to serve in their army. At the time of World War II, Korea was ruled by Japan, and many Koreans were forced to serve in the Imperial Japanese Army. Jastak wasn't all that pleased to be serving as a Japanese soldier, and in particular, he wasn't keen on acting out the brutality that was expected of him. After a couple of weeks of coming to our house, he became more and more friendly, to the point where he began to call Tante Marie, "Mama," and freely showed all of us pictures of his family on their farm back in Korea.

In the meantime, Tante Marie's two daughters, Corrie and Olga, returned from our grandparent's home in Trawas where they lived for the first part of the war. Corrie and Olga had learned to speak quite a bit of Japanese when they were in Trawas, so they were able to converse with Jastak, which helped to further the relationship between our family and "the enemy." Eventually, Jastak called Tante Marie *"Mama Besar,"* which means "big mama," and he called my mother *"Mama Ketjiel,"* which means "small mama."

Jastak was a guard for the prisoners who worked the gardens at the ravine. There were other guards who would come to our house also. One was Onok and another was Kanada, and they were also conscripted Korean soldiers. Kanada was a bigger man and he and Jastak didn't get along at all, and I'll tell more about that later.

About 50 to 60 POWs worked on the gardens in the ravine and the Japanese soldiers guarded them. Tante Marie arranged so she was allowed to make tea for the prisoners in the afternoon after they had finished working for the day. I helped to distribute the tea, which was made in huge pans that were given to us by the Japanese. I was allowed to ladle the tea out to the prisoners as they came by. There was no food of course, because we didn't have food to give away, but we did make tea for them, and the cost for this came out of our pocket. The prisoners would come up on the street after their workday was finished, and line up in formation in front of our house. Each had his own plate and a cup. After a while, some of the neighbors began to contribute toward the tea, and it became more of a neighborhood endeavor.

In addition, however, when the neighbors began contributing toward this effort, they began trying to smuggle notes and food into the camps for their loved ones. Tante Marie had taken a leadership role in giving tea to the prisoners. This led the townspeople to think she had some sort of "in" with the camps, and they brought her things they wanted smuggled into the camps. Tante Marie would have none of this and refused all requests. It was dangerous for anyone trying to smuggle things into the camps, and it was trouble for the prisoner also, because there could be terrible punishment if they were discovered.

The soldiers had built a sort of tower made out of bamboo in the middle of the ravine. It was a watch tower to keep an eye on the prisoners as they worked, and it was as tall as a tree. Kanada allowed Huibert and me to climb the tower sometimes and I felt like I could see forever.

I liked Kanada because he said nice things to me, and called me a "big boy" and said I was "stout," which made me proud. He always walked around with his bayonet attached to his belt and one day he took off his belt and put it on me. I felt so proud walking around with that scary bayonet that almost reached the floor. I was ready to run off to find Huibert and my friends to show them how grown up I was and how I looked in the heavy belt, but someone stopped me before I could get out the door. That was a good thing because I don't think Kanada would have been happy to see me run away with his bayonet.

One day one of the prisoners started singing as he worked. The man had a beautiful strong voice and sang opera music as good as could be heard on any stage. Kanada liked the music and encouraged the man to keep singing while the other prisoners did the work. In fact, Kanada allowed the man to climb the tower so he could be better heard. He sang "O Sole Mio," from the top of the tower, and the sound flowed over the entire neighborhood. It was truly beautiful.

After doing this a few times, Kanada, who knew the music and obviously thought he was as good a singer as the prisoner, sent the man back to work and began to sing the same opera music himself from atop the tower. There was no comparison, of course, and Kanada's voice, along with his Korean/Japanese accent, was almost comical. Nevertheless, no one dared to say or do anything that might upset the guard. We just listened and tried to imagine it was the prisoner singing.

Jastak and Kanada didn't get along well; it was just one of those things where they didn't argue or anything we could see, but they gave off vibes which said they didn't like each other. Then came the day when we heard noises outside in front of the house. There was yelling and grunting and thumping. We ran to see what was happening, and there they were, punching each other, rolling over and over on the big rocks and in the sharp thorny weeds alongside the road. Noses were bleeding and they were scratched and bruised all over. Tante Marie came to the front porch and started yelling at them to stop. Another guard came over and with the butt of his big rifle he separated them.

Both came to our house to get cleaned up. Kanada went to the back bathroom outside, and Jastak was inside in our bathroom. All of a sudden I heard a sharp slap, and Tante Marie yelling in Indonesian, "Why did you have to fight?!" Slap! "Don't you think there's enough fighting already?!" Slap! And on it went. I crept by the door and saw her yelling and slapping Jastak on his bald head while he bent in front of her trying to wash his face in the sink. He was cringing and saying, "Sorry Mama, sorry Mama, I won't do it again ..." and she would yell and slap him again while putting ointment on his cuts.

I can't help but think now, years later, what a chance Tante Marie was taking by befriending Jastak. She was deliberately thumbing her nose at the Imperial Japanese Emperor's representative to whom we were supposed to bow, not chastise. Only Tante Marie could get away with such actions.

Not long after this incident, the Japanese army began to store things in the back of our house in the yard. There were supplies and equipment for the work being done in the ravine, and some food, like sweet potatoes and rice. Jastak told Tante Marie our family could use some of the supplies if we needed them. I'm sure Tante Marie didn't abuse the privilege, but I'm also sure she did give some food, scarce as it was, to people who needed it.

At the end of every workday, the prisoners brought their equipment and supplies to the back yard, and what needed to be protected from the rain was put under the roof. All was supervised, usually by Jastak. One day I heard voices way in the back of the house and I went to see what was going on.

There stood Jastak, who had just dropped his pants and was standing in his underwear, a sort of loincloth. Tante Marie was beside him with her arms full of clothing; his uniform on one arm and civilian clothes on the other arm. He began to dress with a full set of civilian clothes underneath, and then they put his uniform on over the civilian clothes. Once dressed, he went back to the camps where he somehow managed to secretly get the clothes to prisoners in need.

I learned later that wasn't the only time he did this, and between Jastak and Tante Marie, they smuggled many pieces of clothing into the camps for desperate POWs. I have no idea what else they might have smuggled in or out of the camps, but it was extremely dangerous and Jastak put himself in serious jeopardy every time he did it.

Thinking about all of this later, I don't know how they concocted this idea. Somehow I guess because of Jastak's high regard for Tante Marie, over time he really felt like a son to her. He came every day to the house, no longer to take naps, but just to visit.

Another thing I learned about Jastak was that he "pretended" to beat prisoners. He told Tante Marie the guards were required to periodically beat prisoners for no real reason. If the guards didn't do this, they were penalized and they came under suspicion for being sympathizers and getting soft. They were made to find insignificant reasons to flog prisoners to maintain their superiority and keep prisoners submissive. Jastak chose specific prisoners who knew him, and when he would rise above them shouting and menacing, they would cower. Jastak would gently knock them to the ground and pretend to kick them, all the while cursing and yelling loudly. In the end, the prisoners were not hurt, but Jastak's supervisors were satisfied that he was being sufficiently cruel.

Learning to fish

At the bottom of the ravine there was a small stream. The Japanese had dammed up the water and created a little pond and stocked it with fish. Before long, the little pond was way overcrowded. I believe the ultimate idea was the fish could be eaten, but I don't know if it was a good type of fish to eat, and people didn't seem to be eating them. They might have been some type of goldfish which are not good to eat.

One day close to the end of the war, Kanada told Huibert to find a bamboo stick, some sewing thread, and a needle and he would teach us to fish. He tied the thread onto the stick, bent the needle, and put a tiny piece of sweet potato on the end. He dropped it into the pond and immediately caught a fish and it whizzed out of the water. He did it again, and right away, whoop, out came a fish, about six inches long. He soon had a little pile of fish beside him and then Huibert tried it. It didn't take much longer before he caught several fish, too. Eventually they didn't even need the sweet potato on the end of the needle.

To my reluctant dismay, my turn came next. Actually, I was scared to death I might catch one. I really didn't want to do this, but it was expected I should at least try. I gingerly put the hook into the water and waited and waited, and nothing happened. Not a single bite and I thought I was doing exactly what the others had done. I stood there some more, and finally I just pulled the pole up and walked away.

That was the beginning and the end of my fishing adventures. I never to this day have tried to catch a fish again. I eat fish when they are put on my plate, yes, but I leave it to someone else to catch them.

I've often wondered about those fish, because to my knowledge, we never ate one. When they stocked the pond the Japanese might have thought they were good to eat, but I know they were not. One possibility is the fish might have been ground up and used for fertilizer. Another is they were taken back to feed prisoners at the camps. Bad as they were, those people were desperate for food and might have eaten them. I just don't know the answer to it.

The war comes to an end

Jastak came to us one day and told us the war was ending. There was no public news published at that time, and all information was shared person to person by gossip, rumor, or hearsay only. We were not allowed to have radios. All of them had been confiscated along with any other hi-tech equipment or machines we might have had at the beginning of the war. The only newspaper available was Japanese, and the news was always in their favor. We heard daily they had dealt the Americans another severe blow and had the Allied Forces on the run.

Whenever the Japanese were dealt a harsh defeat with a large loss of troops, other units of their army would come through the city at night. They would march in the dark and sing songs of mourning which sounded eerily somber. We learned to recognize those songs and we knew they had been defeated in a battle somewhere. The propaganda, however, always announced the Japanese were winning the war. Eventually, there was more and more nightly singing and we knew things were not going well for them.

When Jastak came the last time to see us, he told Tante Marie he would soon be going home. He asked her what she was going to do after the liberation. When she said she didn't know, he offered to take our whole family back to Korea to live on the farm with his family. He was tearful and worried about what would happen to us if we stayed. There was no doubt he was sincere in his efforts to save us, but Tante Marie and my mother were just as sincere about staying in Bandung until my father could find us when he was freed. Jastak's kind offer was gently refused and we never saw him again.

When Jastak left, the prisoners didn't come anymore and we didn't see the Japanese guards, but otherwise, life went on in pretty much the same way. We just continued to live day to day.

Somehow Huibert and I had found an old BB gun. It was not very strong or accurate, but it was a BB gun. We were walking around with the gun one day and soon a bunch of Indonesian boys came around. We were looking for birds or something to shoot. We never could have shot anything because the BB gun was so bad, but we tried. Suddenly one of the boys yelled, "Aim for that – aim for that!" He was looking at the sky and there was a lot of noise from an airplane we had never seen before. It had Dutch colors on the side and on the tail and we were confused and wondered why the Japanese would have that sort of plane.

The plane flew over downtown Bandung and dropped crates of food. We watched in astonishment as it turned around and made another pass and dropped more crates. It turned out to be a B-25 Mitchell Bomber from the Dutch Air Force, and it most likely came from Australia with food supplies from the Allies.

In this simple and unofficial way we learned about the surrender of the Japanese and the beginning of our liberation and restoration. But, little did we know at the time, it was also the beginning of the worst and darkest part of the war. The *Bersiap* had begun.

Chapter 3

The Bersiap

Surrender

The Japanese surrendered to the Allies on August 15, 1945. As there was no Allied re-conquest of Indonesia, the Japanese were still in charge and had received specific orders to maintain the status quo until Allied Forces arrived.

Sukarno,[7] Mohammad Hatta, and other native leaders were hesitant to act because they did not want to provoke conflict with the Japanese. Vice Admiral Maeda Tadashi, an Imperial Japanese Navy officer in Jakarta, was responsible for transferring political power, and he wanted a quick transfer of power to the older generation of Indonesian leaders. However, he feared the volatile militant youth groups because of how badly the Japanese had treated large numbers of natives during the occupation.

While the older nationalist leadership group were reluctant, younger members of the new elite, the youth (Indonesian: *pemuda*), wanted to push for revolution. A group of them kidnapped Sukarno and Hatta and forced them to declare Indonesian independence. On August 17, 1945, two days after the Japanese surrender, Sukarno and

---

[7] **Sukarno**, born **Kusno Sosrodihardjo** (June 6, 1901–June 21, 1970) was the first President of Indonesia. He spoke fluent Dutch and went to the University at Delft in Holland.

Hatta declared independence at Sukarno's house in Jakarta. Their public statement was:

Proclamation
We the People of Indonesia hereby declare the
Independence of Indonesia.
Matters which concern the transfer of power
and other things will be executed by careful means and
in the shortest possible time.
Jakarta, 17 August 1945
In the name of the People of Indonesia
Sukarno – Hatta

Indonesian staff briefly seized Jakarta radio from their Japanese supervisor and broadcast the news of the declaration across Java. The following day, Sukarno was declared President and Hatta was Vice President of the newly announced Republic of Indonesia.

It was mid-September before news of the declaration of independence spread to the outer islands, and many Indonesians far from the capital of Jakarta did not believe it. As the news expanded, a small percentage of Indonesians came to regard themselves as pro-Republic, and they inspired a mood of revolution to sweep across the country. External power had shifted. It would be weeks before Allied Forces entered Indonesia, and the Dutch were too weakened by World War II to reclaim their colony. Imprisoned Dutch officials were just coming out of POW camps in dreadful condition, and leadership of the country as it was conducted prior to the war, was impossible.

The Japanese, on the other hand, were required by the terms of the surrender to both lay down their arms and maintain order, a contradiction which some resolved by handing weapons to Japanese-trained Indonesians. At the time of the surrender, there were 70,000 Japanese troops in Java and Sukarno and Hatta were concerned that independence celebration rallies would result in the guns of Japanese troops being turned on Indonesian crowds.

The resulting power vacuum in the weeks following the Japanese surrender created an atmosphere of uncertainty, but also one of opportunity for the pro-Republicans. While the older leadership set about constructing a government on paper, they could do little to stop younger mobs. These *pemuda* rebels attacked members of the Indonesian elite, retaliated violently against those village heads who had assisted Japanese oppression of Indonesian peasants, and fought for turf and weapons. Next on their list of "oppressors" were the Dutch, Indos, and other Europeans, and revolution began.

Bersiap is the name given by the Dutch to the violent and chaotic period of the Indonesian National Revolution following the end of World War II. The Indonesian word *bersiap* means "get ready" or "be prepared."

Records say the *Bersiap* period lasted from August 1945 to December 1946, and the majority of the violence, particularly against Indos, occurred on the island of Java. The death toll of the *Bersiap* period ran into tens of thousands of Indos alone, and because of issues including lack of communication in remote villages, true numbers will never be known. According to Wikipedia®, the bodies of 3,600 Indo-Europeans were officially identified as killed. However more than 20,000 registered Indo-European civilians were abducted and never seen again.

I have learned the worst place during the *Bersiap* was in eastern Java, in the Surabaya area and the city of Malang where I was born. People were indiscriminately slaughtered there by the hundreds, by rebels. But, living in Bandung and then Jakarta, we were not aware of these atrocities while they were occurring.

The period ended with the departure of the British military in 1946, by which time the Dutch had rebuilt their military capacity. Meanwhile, the Indonesian revolutionary fighters were well into the process of forming a formal military, and the last Japanese troops were evacuated by July 1946.

My story continues

Soon after the strange planes dropped crates of food and supplies for survivors, cars were driving all around town with the Indonesian flag waving and people draped all over the car yelling, "*Merdeka, Merdeka!*" This means "freedom," but more specifically, Indonesian freedom. Unbeknownst to us, Sukarno had already been proclaiming independence for Indonesia, and the Japanese had authorized him to do that.

We learned in the *Merdeka* negotiations that Sukarno had forbidden Indonesians to trade with the Dutch. Without notice, the markets were closed to the Dutch and we couldn't buy any food. This was devastating to everyone, but as God provides, one day a Japanese guard who used to come to our house, came in civilian clothes and brought us tofu. We were shocked and had no money to pay, but he didn't want money. He gave us the tofu and offered to bring us more food, also.

At the same time, the POWs were being let out of the camps. The ones who were local and lived in the area just dragged themselves to their homes. Two of the dozens of prisoners who had been working in the ravine came one day to our house to thank my mother and Tante Marie for their kindness in giving them tea in the afternoons. It was good to see them free, and it was comical too, because one day two hugely tall Dutchmen came riding up to our house on a tiny little motorcycle, probably 100 cc. It was important for them to do this, and it was certainly kind of them to remember us in the midst of their excitement at being free.

The Japanese are gone

Almost overnight everything changed when the Japanese disappeared. Short-lived as it turned out to be, there was an aura of freedom as we began to realize we were no longer under their rule. Even with the shortage of food and supplies, there was a feeling of liberty around us.

One of the first prisoners to return was Mrs. Tegelaar's Dutch husband. She was the lady with TB who lived with us in Mrs. Allirol's house. One day, to the joy of his wife and son, Mr. Tegelaar came walking up to the house. The next morning his wife decided to fix him a precious egg as a special treat for his breakfast, believing he might not have had access to eggs while in prison. She remembered how he liked them, and carefully prepared him a perfectly fried egg. When she proudly brought the small plate to the table, he took one look at the egg and pronounced it was too soft. Mrs. Tegelaar dutifully took it back to the kitchen and a few minutes later brought it to him again with a smile on her face. He pronounced it too hard. The smile disappeared and for the first time I saw tears on her face.

This story brings many questions to mind as to how Mr. Tegelaar might have spent the war, and also why he was among the very first people allowed to leave the camps, as it was many days and even weeks before we saw anyone else come back. All of this is a mystery, however, and the fried egg and Mrs. Tegelaar's tears are all I remember about Mr. Tegelaar's return. Very soon the family packed up and left.

Another move

The house we lived in on Ring Boulevard that belonged to Mrs. Allirol had an empty lot next to it, and next to the lot was another house that had a second floor. This was unusual in Indonesia because most houses were one story. The huge two story house was occupied by one Japanese man. He was called a civilian, but was actually a highly placed Japanese bureaucrat who helped to run the city and its economic system. The man had a car and chauffeur, and a large staff of mostly Indonesian women to run the household. When the war ended, the house emptied overnight. After a while, the owner appeared at our door and asked us to move in so it wouldn't remain empty and vulnerable to damage. Tante Marie and her daughters Olga and Corrie, and Oom Ben moved there with my mother, Huibert, and me.

Bersiap atrocities

In later years I learned more about some of the atrocities of the *Bersiap* period, the terrifying time between August 1945 and when it is recognized that the *Bersiap* ended, December 1946. The ending date is not realistic, as small bands of rebels were known to be active for several years after 1946, and certain areas of Java, particularly, were not safe to travel.

Things were even worse in East Java as far as random killings and assaults on people of European descent than they were in West Java where we lived. My cousin Humphrey, the son of my mother's brother Willie, lived in East Java, near Surabaya, and he was put in jail by the Indonesian rebels. There was no reason for him to be arrested, but the rebels in that area were even more radical than in West Java, and captured and imprisoned people for reasons as simple as not being full Indonesian. This was a regular jail rather than a prison camp, and there were many people incarcerated there. Food was scarce and much appreciated when it came.

One day when the prisoners were about to get their meager evening meal, they heard shouting. Humphrey looked out his cell window and saw a Japanese man in full battle dress crouching atop the prison wall. He was shouting loudly, "Don't eat the food – don't eat the food! All of the food is poisoned!" As hard as it was to turn down the food which came soon after, no one ate it. That very evening when most likely all of the prisoners doubted whether the food was really bad, they were liberated from the jail by the Japanese, their former enemy. As the story ends, they learned the food really was poisoned and all would have died if they had eaten it.

While we were enjoying our first taste of freedom after seeing crates of food being dropped and the Japanese were no longer on our street, the *Bersiap* rebellion had already started within the city. There were riots, and the Indonesian rebels found cars and packed them with young men and drove around the city. We saw them driving by and didn't realize what they were doing. They were shaking their fists at us and yelling like crazy, so we waved happily and shook our fists, too, as they drove by with Indonesian flags flying.

Then things turned ugly. The men were not yet back from the camps and there were many women alone and women with children, with no one to defend them. The British had moved in to try to maintain law and order, but in the whole city there were very few British troops. In fact, the numbers of British troops in all of Indonesia were grossly inadequate to handle the violence.

There were vicious attacks by the Indonesian rebels on groups of people everywhere, whom they thought to be Dutch or Indo. Rebels would accost people in the street and before anyone realized, they murdered them. They ransacked houses, smashed in doors to take anything they wanted, and brutalized the people.

Rebels in our home

Before any troops, British or otherwise, had been organized to adequately patrol or watch neighborhoods, our house was attacked by a group of rebels. We were not as unfortunate as some other families, but it was a frightening thing to happen all the same.

When we lived in the two-story house, I developed a case of the chicken pox and had spots all over my body. I didn't feel sick, but the doctor wanted me to stay in bed, or at least in my room. One day when I was lying in bed and wishing I could be outside, I heard some loud commotion downstairs and my mother ran in my room very quickly and out of breath. She dumped a load of jewelry and other valuables under the covers on my bed. She also hung our worthless BB gun on the bedpost.

A group of fearsome rebels, about seven or eight of them, had unexpectedly stormed in the house, frightening everyone nearly to death. A friend of the family was visiting at the time, an Indo man who often came by to do things for us. The rebels demanded everyone in the house to line up against the wall with their hands up, and two of them pressed their sharpened bamboo spears against Oom Ben and the visitor's hearts. The others yelled something about a gun and began searching, streaming in and out of every corner of the house.

A moment later, an Indonesian man wielding a gun appeared in the doorway to my room. He yelled excitedly, "There it is! There it is!" while pointing to the BB gun hanging on my bedpost. At the same time, he saw my face covered in chicken pox, and he stopped in his tracks and wouldn't come near the bed. We'll never know if he really got a good look at the worthless gun, or his fear of catching the disease wouldn't let him continue his search. He said loudly, "That can't be it!" and he immediately turned around and stomped downstairs.

Almost as suddenly as they stormed our house, the frightening rebels left us and went on to terrorize our neighbors.

Later, we heard someone claimed there had been shots fired from our direction into the *kampong* nearby, and that's why the rebels were searching the houses for a gun. I suspect my mother's quick thinking and the Indonesians' innate fear of any sort of pox saved our lives that day.

Enemy/protector

Some of the British troops to attempt to maintain law and order were *Gurkas*, a type of Mongolian Buddhist people. These men were known as good fighters. They carried huge knives, sort of like a Bowie knife, with an angle in the blade, almost like a boomerang. The claim was they could throw those knives like a boomerang which would do their damage, and come back to the men who threw them. I never saw it happen, but scuttlebutt among the boys in the neighborhood said it did. We were always happy to see the *Gurkas* because they made us feel safer.

The British drafted some of the Japanese soldiers who had been put in the camps when the other people were liberated. They carved the neighborhoods up into small areas and put a contingency of about 12 Japanese men in charge of patrolling each area. They gave them back their rifles and told them they were now responsible for the safety of the people and to maintain civility in these areas. Even though there were hardly enough of them to completely control the rebels, it did help. Our enemy had become our protector.

Huibert was witness to a curious incident in Bandung. This was early in the *Bersiap* period, before we really knew what was actually happening because we didn't have newspapers or radio or official news of any kind. At the time some of the Japanese were walking free in Bandung. We didn't know why they were not in the camp where we thought they were supposed to be, but they were walking free.

Huibert, who was about 13 years old by this time, had gone to the barber one day, where we always went in Bandung, to get his hair cut. This was an Indonesian barber shop and while he was sitting in the barber chair, a commotion began in the street. Suddenly the Indonesian barber, who knew our family well, took a little red and white Indonesian flag pin from off his lapel and put it on Huibert's lapel. He then shoved Huibert under a small table near the window so they could protect him. Huibert looked from under the table and saw people running outside and a lot of action. He crawled out and watched out the window with the other people from the shop and they saw a bunch of Indonesian youths chasing a Japanese soldier. The rebels had machetes and one of them started to hit the man. They did wound him in the head, but the Japanese man was able to wrestle the machete away from the boy. He escaped toward the direction of the camp, streaming blood from the wound in his head all the way.

Huibert jumped on his bicycle and raced home to tell us about what was happening. We finally put two and two together and realized the men we had seen driving around town with the flags waving with whom we smilingly shook our fists in the air, were the rebels who were attacking people all over the city.

This incident, and many more like it, was what triggered the

British to arm the Japanese to help patrol and protect the city. In addition to the rifles given to the Japanese, they had armored trucks they used to patrol the streets. These had an opening in the top where the driver looked out of bullet-proof glass. They were called "Panser wagens," and they carried armed soldiers inside.

With the Japanese helping the British deal with lawlessness, most of the violence in the city of Bandung was stopped within a day. The Japanese told the British if they could do this in a day in Bandung, to give them two weeks and they could stop the violence in the rest of Java, referring to the more violent actions which were happening particularly in East Java at the time. The British didn't go for this and we'll never know whether thousands of lives might have been saved if they had.

Instead, the Brits started outposts around the city of Bandung and maintained them with Japanese soldiers who kept watch and control of the rebels and protected the citizens as best they could.

More struggles to survive

Meanwhile, food was scarce and getting scarcer. Sukarno had forbidden trading for food or other goods between the Indonesians and the Dutch or Indos.

Behind a high fence on the open lot behind our house was a well-tended vegetable garden, and there was a tiny bamboo house there where a young Indonesian man lived with his wife and child.

We had made his acquaintance when we lived in Mrs. Allirol's house before we moved to the two-story house. The young man had come to our back door and asked my mother if we had any medication because his child was sick. The only medication we had in the house was a few aspirin tablets. My mother had compassion on the young man and gave him a couple of aspirins and told him how to give them to the child. He was very thankful. He might have come back one more time for more aspirin, but other than that, we never saw him again.

Now we were living in the two-story house, and one day I was looking out my second floor bedroom window at the wall which surrounded our house. The wall had barbed wire on top which the Japanese diplomat had installed when he occupied the house. Suddenly I saw a hand at the top of the wall, pushing the barbed wire up, and the hand held a basket which was being tipped toward our house. Out of the basket rolled ears of corn, sweet potatoes, cucumbers, and other vegetables, onto the ground. It was food – precious food – being shared by our neighbor who lived in the little bamboo hut. No doubt he knew about the food shortages and the lack of trading, and he was showing his thanks for my mother helping his sick child all that time before. We were thrilled and thankful for the food and the generous amount of it. He did this at least one more time several weeks later.

Because we had moved and Mrs. Allirol was alone now in her house, Oom Ben gave her a horn to honk if there was trouble or if she felt unsafe. It was the sort of horn you might see on a motorcycle, where you pinched a rubber ball, and the horn sounded.

Not long after this in the middle of the night, I woke up and my mother was looking out the window. It was pitch dark, and she had a five-gallon metal can she was banging on with a big wooden spoon, and yelling, "*Maling, maling!*" which means "Thief, thief!" Besides the noise of the yelling and banging, I heard the little horn from Mrs. Allirol, going "beep, beep, beep." She was also yelling "Thief, thief," and I expect it woke up the whole neighborhood.

A couple of nights later the same thing happened; the horn was going "beep, beep, beep," and my mother was leaning out the window yelling "*Maling, maling!*" Apparently some men were trying to break into Mrs. Allirol's house and she was having none of it and was yelling and beeping as loud as she could.

To safeguard our few valuables, and our lives as well, we put anything we had on the second floor, and we slept there, too. We then built an elaborate system to block the stairway with ladders and furniture. We had bottles of water lined up to eventually use as projectiles in case someone did break in. We also got assigned guard duty where we stayed awake through the night to watch for problems, and everyone had to take a turn. When it was my turn, I sat there watching the back wall intently. It got so I expected something to happen and I'm sure I saw things in the night that weren't really there. It was a scary time.

Behind us there was a row of houses and the lot where the Indonesian man had his little bamboo house and his big garden. The day after the second yelling and beeping incident, the farmer came to us and said he had heard some sort of dangerous rumor in the *kampong* that we should stop sounding the alarm. Actually, it was a "soft threat."

It turned out the young farmer was the ring-leader of a group of men who were looting some of the houses. We didn't think they would have disturbed our house because my mother had helped him with his baby so long ago, but the implication was definite. It would be wise if we stopped sounding the alarm in the middle of the night so his little band of thieves could go about their business of looting the other houses in the neighborhood.

After the warning for us to stop sounding the alarm, which we did, the food supply stopped coming over the back wall. We missed the food, of course, but we were also not attacked or broken into by his group, and this was appreciated.

There was an organization called RAPWI, Rehabilitation of Allied Prisoners of War and Internees (the Prisoners of War were military people, and the internees were everyone else who got put in the camps). The organization was kind of like the Red Cross and it dealt with registration of people and they distributed food. Many of the people who had been held in the camps were still in the camps. They were able to come and go to try to find their relatives and such, and a good number of them went home if they were from the area. However, many of the prisoners had been sent to Bandung from other cities and islands, and they had no way to get to their homes. Many of them were also weak and sick and needed help.

Staying in the camps was a form of safety, and they weren't strong enough to leave.

The RAPWI group helped people, but the rebels were more and more in the open as time went on. There was increasing unrest and gangs were roaming through the city. The RAPWI people drove around the city in cars trying to establish their presence and keep the peace as best they could.

Even though we were living in the two-story house with the knowledge of the owner, it didn't belong to us, and we were soon assigned a house by RAPWI. The assigned house was close to the downtown area and the market where I used to go with Maktje. It had also been part of one of the camps where women and children were kept during the war. We decided to move to where we were supposed to go.

Somehow a truck became available and we loaded up some small furniture and things like pots and pans. I went along with the first load delivered to the house. It was a small house with a tiny yard, and we delivered the first load of our belongings, and came back to get the second.

We saw a lot of commotion at the house when we returned, people mingling around and they seemed to be upset. We asked what was happening, and they said they were delaying the move. We asked why, and the answer was, "We have just been attacked!"

A gang had come from across the ravine from the *kampong*, and they took some pot shots at our neighborhood. One of the men, who was living behind us, was not afraid. In the middle of the attack, he marched up to the Japanese post and told the officer in charge they had just been attacked. The Japanese officer could have said something like, "Well, why do you come to me? You should go to the British."

Instead, the Japanese soldiers took their job seriously, and two of them came in full battle dress, and marched smartly in front of our house. One of them took control and ordered the other to stop, and on his command, both put their bayonets on their rifles. Click.

The one in command yelled "Charge!" and they ran down the ravine yelling in their blood-curdling guttural roar all the way to meet the enemy. They had no idea how many rebels were awaiting them, but it was no matter to them; they were in full battle-cry and eager to uphold their newly acquired duty of protecting us.

When the rebels saw the soldiers in their storming attack, the banana trees began to sway and the bushes trembled as dozens of them crawled out of their hiding places, and ran as fast as they could to get away.

Upon gaining the top of the ravine on the other side and seeing not a single rebel remaining, the soldiers marched back the way they came, and walked up to our house. Our fearless Tante Marie met them at the door. The two formidable soldiers asked her politely if they could have a glass of water. Request granted. Each got his glass of water and they marched back to their post.

The move was then called off completely as there was unrest everywhere, and we found out it was particularly bad in the neighborhood of the house to which we were supposed to move. We never got our first load of belongings back which we had already moved, because it was just too dangerous to return. I guess it was the price we had to pay to find out we didn't want to live in that area, and we never went back there.

Another family from our street did complete their move to the area in the south near the little house that we were going to occupy. In fact, just prior to our halted move, they used the same truck with which we made the one trip. This was a woman and her mother and her two sons who lived near us on Ring Boulevard. The sons, Karl and Pete Termeitelen, were older than we were, but we played with them sometimes, and they were a nice family.

Oom Ben told Mrs. Termeitelen she shouldn't make the move because of the danger. She was not convinced and said she wanted to be with all of her furniture and possessions which had already been moved, and she wasn't going to change her mind.

Division of the city

Things went from bad to worse when the British decided to cut Bandung in half. The railroad was the line of demarcation. South of the railroad tracks was considered Indonesian territory and was controlled by the rebel army. North of the tracks, or at least a large piece of the northern area, was where most Indos and Europeans, including us, already lived. This area included the airport, and there was a huge villa on the road to Lembang that was occupied by British troops, so things were fairly safe there. The new house on the mountain which we never occupied was completely lost to us now because it was in an area far north of Bandung and under Indonesian rebel control.

The Termeitelen family was trapped in the southern Indonesian-held area. We lost track of them after their move, but much later we heard a son, Pete, went missing during the unrest, and one day he just didn't come home. We believe the rest of the family eventually made it out of the country and went to Holland, but it was years later because Mrs. Termeitelen insisted on staying in case Pete came home. This never happened and, sadly, Pete was forever lost.

Near where we had the garden Huibert and I had taken care of, was a house with another Indo family who had several sons. They were several years older than we were, maybe 17 to 19 or so. One day one of the boys came riding home on a motorcycle. We didn't know how he got it, but he drove around and enjoyed showing off his motorcycle to all the boys in the neighborhood. As boys will do, he made a wager with someone. He bragged that he could ride his motorcycle across the railroad tracks into the southern Indonesian controlled territory. He might have done this once already and thought he could get away with it again. However, this time it didn't work. The young man and his motorcycle didn't make it back over the tracks, and neither was ever seen again.

The British had taken control of one of the schools – the Lyceum – as a base for their military camp. It was close to a hospital, too, and the area was well guarded. I don't understand the thinking of the rebels, but they attacked from the east at the edge of town and started to fire on the hospital. The guards there were battle-hardened British, armed to the hilt, and the rebels stormed the school and the hospital. They did it to terrorize the people, which they certainly did, but the attack didn't last long before they were driven off.

The rebels did this many times; attacked an area to terrorize the people and take control of it. They were never able to hold any area for long before being driven off, but they created a great deal of chaos and danger.

During the attack on the Lyceum, Oom Ben saw some rebels milling around near our house. He decided it was time for us to get out of our lonely street where we were quite exposed and could be easy pickings for the rebels. He thought there was safety in numbers and we should go to the more populated neighborhood behind us.

We packed up whatever we could carry and Oom Ben urged us to start walking down the street. Fortunately, we carried our mattresses on our backs and when we heard shots coming from behind us, we cut through the garden of the long-gone Indonesian farmer and stepped up our pace, while dodging rebel bullets.

Dangerous? Absolutely! And whether it was nervous exhaustion, terrified energy, or whatever it might be called, Huibert and I actually giggled a little as we thought how silly we must look galloping along with our mattresses covering our heads, and bullets flying all around us.

Our little group at that time included my mother, Huibert and me, plus Tante Marie and Corrie and Olga, and Oom Ben. We made it safely to the house of some friends, who took us in. This was the home of the Bowens, a Dutch mother whose military husband was still in the camps, and her two sons and daughter. We stayed there for several days.

Mrs. Bowens knew an Indonesian woman, Mrs. Haring, who lived nearby in a huge house on the corner of two streets. She was the wife of a well-educated and wealthy man who had chosen to be on the side of Sukarno during the *Bersiap*. The man and his sons left to serve with the Indonesian Army in Jogjakarta, while the woman and her daughters stayed in Bandung and sympathized with the Indos.

It was safer in this more populated neighborhood and Mrs. Haring opened her house to all of us, the Bowens family and ours. Even though the house was very large with many rooms, I know Oom Ben, Huibert, and I, plus one of the Bowens boys all slept in one room. The very first night in this house was wonderful for me – I felt safe and could sleep through the night. No guard duty and no beeping and yelling, plus no dodging bullets. It was truly a relief.

There was a police station across the street and Oom Ben soon decided to return to being a police captain, which he had been prior to the war. The safety we felt when we saw Oom Ben in his new uniform with a huge revolver, was comforting. We all felt we could breathe freely again.

After about a week or so, Oom Ben went back to the two-story house to get some of our things. However, after we left, a group of British troops had moved in and they refused us access. Later, Oom Ben went to a higher official and he was able to go into the house, but by that time many of our picture albums were ripped to pieces and some other things were destroyed. Also, the Brits had given away some of our belongings including our pots and pans, to people in the house behind us. Oom Ben went to the house and asked for our things back and actually saw some of our possessions there, but the people refused to give them back. They claimed because we had left the house, our belongings were "spoils of the war," and besides, they were given to them by the Brits. Our possessions were lost.

My father's return

One day while playing outside, my mother called us into the house. We didn't want to go because we were having fun, but we reluctantly left our play. I mumbled and wondered what my mother wanted now, and slowly opened the door. There stood my father with a big smile on his face.

I was shocked to see him and, in fact, I almost didn't recognize him, except for his wonderful smile. He was very thin and also very dark because he had worked outside so much when he was in the camps. This happened to be on January 24, 1946, my Oom Ben's birthday, and it became a rousing double celebration with my father's return.

How my father got back to us is quite a story.

The last camp where he was imprisoned was on the island of Sumatra. It was liberated by the British and then came under Dutch command. The prisoners had not yet been moved from the camp when word came they were going to be attacked by a huge faction of Indonesian rebels. This was at the beginning of the *Bersiap,* and rumor was that up to 3,000 rebel troops had been assembled into a well-trained army equipped with weapons, and they were going to attack the camp.

The POWs, besides being weakened by hunger and long captivity, had no weapons whatsoever. Everyone began to feverously fashion any sort of weapons they could, such as swords and knives. My father forged by hand a long knife made out of steel that came from the springs of a car. The knife had a wooden handle and a beautiful leather case, which he also made by hand.

After all the hurried preparations, the attack didn't happen. Instead, plans were made to take the prisoners back to Java. All of the military prisoners were put aboard a ship and it sailed toward Jakarta. However, there was a change in orders stating prisoners were not allowed to disembark in Jakarta, even after the ship had docked. The plan was to return immediately to Sumatra.

My father and his good friend, Dick Brinkman, who had stuck together through the whole war, were determined they would not return to the miserable camps in Sumatra. The dangers there were enormously great. They were now almost within sight of home and there was no telling when – or if – they might come back. It was time for drastic action.

They basically jumped ship in Jakarta, like something out of the movies. As the ship pulled into the harbor and the gangplank lowered, they had some other men distract the guards, and shortly before the ship was to leave again, the two of them took their meager belongings and stole away down the plank. They hid in some harbor warehouses for a while because the harbor was about 20 miles away from the city, and everything was then controlled by the rebels.

Pa and Dick were sneaking around the warehouses trying to figure out how to get a ride to Jakarta, when suddenly my father saw a man he knew. Not only was it someone he knew, the man had a truck! Pa waved him down and told him their story. They clambered on the truck and after some discussion the man took them to the military base in Jakarta because they were still officially members of the military.

Once on the army base my father formally announced he was Sergeant van Demmeltraadt reporting for duty. Surprised, the officials said, "Well, what are you doing here? You don't belong here." They went on to complain they didn't have enough food and space for extra people. My father replied, "Well, what should I do, sleep in the street, or what? I'm a military man and I've been released from the POW camp, and I don't know what to do."

The army finally allowed both of them to stay on the base, and my father worked as a mechanic on military cars, trucks, and equipment.

About a month later he ran into a friend from pre-war days – J. J. J. de Jong, a handsome and charming guy who had been in a circle of friends with my parents. He was in the Air Force, and at the beginning of the war, when Indonesia was about to surrender to the Japanese, de Jong was sent with a military group to Australia.

His wife and daughters were left behind in Bandung. I heard years later his wife sold things for people during the war to survive, and for everything she sold, she made ten percent. She must have been thrifty, because that ten percent got them safely through the war.

De Jong had been a mechanic like my father, but when he was in Australia, he was sent to the U.S. to get training to become a bomber pilot. Pa and de Jong renewed old acquaintances in Jakarta, and de Jong said he would be flying to Bandung the coming weekend. I found out later he had been making trips to Bandung after the war ended and early in the *Bersiap* period. On one of those trips he found his own family again and took them to safety in Australia.

While in Jakarta, both Dick and my father found out from the Red Cross where their families were living, so when de Jong said he was the co-pilot of a B-25 airplane, and there was a possibility of getting their families out, they decided this was a great idea. Away they flew in a huge B-25 bomber to Bandung.

While they made it to Bandung without incident, the airport of Bandung was out of the city and rebels were hiding along the road, which made local travel dangerous. Because they were military, Pa and Dick somehow commandeered an armored truck and drove it safely to the city, appearing without warning on our doorstep.

My annoyance at being called from play that day was short-lived when I realized who was standing there. With a running leap, I jubilantly vaulted into Pa's arms.

The first thing my father did after hugging us closely, was to check our bodies for signs of disease and vitamin deficiency, like beriberi and rickets. There was a look on my mother's face which could only be pride, when he saw we were healthy.

Flight from Bandung

Conversation was brief on my father's return and the time for rejoicing was yet to come. He told us we had only a short time to gather all our belongings, which weren't many at this point, and we would be leaving in an airplane for Jakarta. Within a day, we packed up everything we had except for our mattresses, which I learned later would have been good to have. After loading Dick's family, too, we headed to the airport in the armored truck.

The plane, which I imagined was the one I had taken pot shots at with my BB gun some weeks before, was huge! I was in total awe at the size of it. Somehow, with me looking up with my mouth open, we climbed the little steps and were in the belly of the beast.

We looked around and there were no seats. What I didn't know at the time of course, was this was just the hull of the B-25. To accommodate the crates of food and supplies dropped on the city by parachute, they took out all of the machine guns from the sides and rear of the plane. But, wherever the machine guns had been were now just openings. There were huge holes along the sides of the plane. The scariest part of all was where they must have pushed out the crates of food. The entire tail of the plane was wide open.

We asked where we should sit, and they said, "Look around and maybe you can sit on one of those tool boxes or on the floor." There was nothing to hang onto – no straps or partitions or pieces sticking out of the wall or anything. We just sat down.

I grabbed a tool box for something to hold onto, sat on it and settled down to listen to the incredible sounds of the plane starting. One engine went around and the plane started shaking, and then the other engine went around and the plane shook some more. The noise grew to become ear-shattering. We started to move and the ground rushed away beside me. We bounced along on an ill-maintained runway that had been full of holes and heaves of concrete from repeated bombings, but was somewhat repaired by the Japanese so they could use it. I held tightly to my equally bouncing tool box. I felt every painful bang on my poorly padded bottom. When I thought it couldn't possibly get any louder, the noise increased ten-fold, and seemed to rip the air apart.

Suddenly the plane lifted off the ground and I thought my heart would leap out of my ears from the noise and the vibration, and from my own sheer excitement. There were no windows in the plane, only the holes. I peeked behind me at the frightening cavernous hole in the tail. There were *sawas* (rice fields) far below, getting smaller and smaller and disappearing as we climbed higher and higher. Soon we were in the clouds, and there came a sort of fog into the plane through the holes and it all became even more eerie.

I peered at the expressions on the faces of the others. They were just sitting there like I was, acting brave. But I know they were just as afraid and excited as I was.

After a long time we landed at the military base, called Tjililitan. This was another scary, first-time adventure seeing the ground approaching through the holes and hearing the noise increasing even more. Feeling the wheels touch the earth was when I finally released my breath, having felt like it was held from the moment I sat down in this monstrous, but fragile flying machine. The military base was surrounded by jungle and it was far away from town, and all of the surrounding territory was under rebel control. Somehow we were safely transported from the Tjililitan to Jakarta. Actually, the rebel violence in Jakarta was quite a bit worse than Bandung. We heard shots every night we lived there, that is when my hearing came back long after the deafening plane ride.

We arrived at a house where my father and Dick had found lodging for all of us. We had two rooms for our family of four, and Dick, and his wife An and their seven-year-old daughter had another room. We had no mattresses for any of us because we hadn't brought them along to Jakarta, but we had bed frames in the house. There were wooden boards on the beds and my mother put all of our clothing on the boards to make a semi-soft area for us to sleep. Over the folded clothes she had a sheet or towels or something. This lasted about a week and somehow they found mattresses for all of us.

Each of the families in the house prepared their own meals and ate together. My mother did the cooking for us, and she bought food wherever she could get it. One day, a doctor who lived in our street looked at the meat a Chinese man was selling door to door. It looked suspicious and after examining it, he determined the meat was human flesh. We had no idea whether we had eaten any or not, but of course we didn't buy any more from him.

We were there only about three weeks and my parents found a bigger place for us. It was on the same street and there was a *kampong* nearby. We rented space in a house belonging to a young Chinese family with one small child and while we were there, the wife gave birth to a daughter. We came to Jakarta in January 1946, and we stayed with the Chinese family until May of that year.

A time of hope

This was a time of expectation, even a time of hope. Although it was not safe in the city, we were reunited as a family and there was some sort of a home life. My father was still in the military and he did have to work at the base. I don't know if he got picked up and dropped off or how he got there, but he did go to work every day. The best part was he came home every night.

J. J. J. de Jong came by to see us frequently between his trips. He was a fantastic story-teller, and I could hardly wait to hear what he had to say. He was a suave and fine-looking man with a tiny mustache, a sharp uniform and a big hat. On his side, he carried a giant Colt 45 with an ivory handle. He smoked just the way Clark Gable smoked, with eyebrows cocked, fingers waving, and smoke wafting around his face. De Jong and some other guys would come in big, mysteriously acquired, military trucks to see us. We would all load in the trucks and go touring and sight-seeing around the city, just to cool off in the heat of the day. Of course everyone had their guns along – just in case.

Everyone in the neighborhood carried a weapon at all times, and Pa carried what was called an Owen gun. This was basically a machine gun which the paratroopers used. I think it was an American gun. It was generally known to be better quality than the British Sten gun, which they called a piece of junk. The Sten guns were quickly made to spit out bullets, with no mention of accuracy. Fortunately, on these touring trips Pa never needed to use his Owen.

Even though horrible things were happening all around me, especially during the *Bersiap*, I was a child who was loved and protected to the best of my family's abilities. I have to say through the whole of World War II, I was blessed with caring adults constantly surrounding me who made my tiny world feel safe. Even though food was often scarce, I don't remember ever being helplessly hungry. For this small thing I will be forever grateful to my mother and Tante Marie, most of all.

Chapter 4

Fleeing to Holland

After the Surrender

Many people were not well coming out of the war. They were either purposely starved and ill-treated in the camps, or hungry because there just wasn't enough food to purchase in the markets. They also had other illnesses acquired from contaminated and unsanitary living conditions. My father, like thousands of others, had contracted malaria in the prison camps in Sumatra.

Holland established a program to help people from Indonesia regain their health and paid to transport them to the Netherlands for access to health care. Also, it was determined that my father could only be discharged from the military in Holland, so it was necessary for him to go there for that reason alone.

My father wrote back and forth to my Oom Anton and Tante Fie (Grandfather van Demmeltraadt's brother and his wife) in Holland, about possibilities of our staying with them if we could get passage. They were happy to have us come and eager to see our family. Because of my father's malaria, our family was given passage. Arrangements were made for us to live with Tante Fie and Oom Anton in one of two small hotels they owned in the city of Zandvoort. This was in the spring of 1946. We left Indonesia on April 27, and arrived in Holland May 24, 1946.

The ship

The trip to Holland was another exciting and well-remembered adventure in my list of "firsts." We lived in Jakarta at the time and the harbor was about 15 miles away. The area was still quite unsafe because of the *Bersiap*. Anyone traveling had to be under armed escort, but I don't really remember the trip to the harbor, which is a good thing. We must have taken some sort of armored truck because there were no buses or public transportation available, and there were other people with us.

Figure 11 The Weltevreden, a converted troop ship that took our family from Indonesia to Holland in May 1946. This picture is from the website of Herman van Oosten, and used with his permission. Over what is called "the first wave" of refugees to Holland from 1945 to 1950, there were 100,000 people transported. Overall, more than 300,000 people were evacuated from Indonesia after WWII. This ship carried 824 passengers on the trip that included our family.

I do remember standing on the dock and looking far up at what was to me an enormous ship. Its name was *Weltevreden* (the word means 'satisfied' in Dutch), and it seemed to go on forever. Walking the gangplank to enter it was exciting. It was actually a small freighter from the Rotterdamsche Lloyd N.V. line. During the war it had been converted to a troop transport, and there was still one cannon on the rear deck. The ship itself was a huge thing, and quite a fascination to me.

Housing on the ship

Girls and boys up to age 12 went with the women, and boys over 12 went with the men. I was coming up to my 11th birthday, so I was put with the women on the ship along with my mother.

The women were housed on multiple levels in the middle of the ship where there was the least turbulence; the men in the front or the bow, and the crew in the back of the ship. Since it was a troop transport and all of the troops in those days were male, there were bunk beds stacked four or five high, and all of the facilities were open and not private at all.

I was assigned to an upper bunk, and to get there, I stepped on the metal frame of each bed and climbed up to my bunk. My mother was in the bunk below mine. The bunks would fold up toward the wall during the day and I don't know where the luggage was kept. It was very hot in the upper bunks, being in the Indian Ocean in May under full sun. There was no air conditioning and little ventilation, so I spent as little time there as I could.

I looked with dismay at the large bathroom facilities, lined with steel walls and floor. The doorways were about a foot off the floor. There were dozens of shower heads on the outside walls, with no division or curtains or anything, and lined up in the middle of the room were the commodes – open seats back to back, only inches apart. However, I learned that sitting there wasn't lonely and there were things to look at – namely a roomful of naked women. Actually, the naked women weren't such a big deal for me. In Indonesia in the *kampongs*, there were many at least half-naked women walking around and doing their chores and such all the time. It was sort of normal to me.

Almost immediately, the floor drains became plugged in the women's section. In the whole big room of commodes and showers, the water sloshed around about ankle deep. It was contained in the facilities area because of the high doorways so at least there was no water in the sleeping area. In the bathroom area, with the ship always in motion, it was quite an adventure to sit on the potty. I learned to raise my feet as the water waved from side to side and from front to back. Whoosh – wave coming – lift the feet. Put the feet down – whoosh – lift the feet again. Not what you would call a tranquil potty sitting …

My mother discovered a small room with somewhat more private bathroom facilities, but when we went there, we found another woman with her two daughters who were my age. There was nothing to do but strip and use the facilities. This was highly uncomfortable for me. I can imagine that it wasn't comfortable for the others either. For me it was worse than the big communal bathroom where there were a lot of women and children of all ages.

Shortly after the start of the journey, my mother got sick with an asthma attack and had to go to the hospital area of the ship. I was alone among all those women so I asked to be put with my father and Huibert in the men's quarters. Thankfully, my request was granted.

My mother was sick for the rest of the journey. In fact, when we did finally dock in Rotterdam, she was hospitalized there and wasn't able to join our family for a couple of weeks.

After the move away from the women's area, I was with the boys and men, and we were in a lower deck than the women. There were about seven decks in all. The sleeping quarters were the same with five-tier bunks against the walls, and the facilities were pretty much the same too, with the commodes all in a row, except now I was looking at naked guys. Many of the men walked around in shoes made of a thick piece of wood attached by a band of rubber cut from an inner tube. This was the forerunner of today's clogs or flip flops, and they were worn by most Indonesians. At least they helped to keep peoples' feet dry.

The floor in the men's area was wet, but it wasn't ankle deep like in the women's area. The floor was made of steel like the rest of the ship, and because the men's facilities were in the front, the floor was severely sloped. One day, one of the boys decided to soap himself all over, and he went to the top of the sloped floor, dropped on his bare slippery bottom and slid down the slope. It didn't take long before we all did this and it was great fun. Unfortunately, it was sort of like a bowling alley; we couldn't stop or steer ourselves very well, and some of the men doing their laundry served as bowling pins. The older boys could better gauge their speed or direction, but on my first trip, I careened smack into a man doing his laundry. His wooden shoes flew in one direction and he flew in another. He tried to grab me but I was all covered in soap and managed to get away to continue improving my sliding skills. A bunch of us boys did this pretty much every afternoon, so before we took a shower, we soaped up and took a couple of slides.

Adventures at sea

The whole experience on the ship was new and every day was exciting. We became quickly accustomed to hearing the drone of the engines and feeling the vibration and the motion 24 hours a day. One day the ship unexpectedly came to an abrupt halt. The motors stopped and all around us was a huge silence. Everyone was looking around at each other wondering what this was. It seemed to happen every three days, and a group of us boys looked around until we found small windows into the engine area. We eventually discovered these stops were when they changed the pistons in the ship's motors. One piston was about seven or eight feet tall, and with the help of a crane they changed them periodically for some sort of maintenance.

When the ship stopped, they also dropped the huge anchors in the front of the ship. When the chains attached to them were loosened, the noise was deafening as the anchors plunged into the sea. Each link in those chains weighed 15 to 20 pounds, and the anchors themselves must have weighed several tons. The chains whizzed around so fast when the anchors dropped that the entire ship shook like a dog shaking water off his back. There was no way the anchors would reach the bottom of the ocean wherever we stopped, but apparently just hanging there was enough to stabilize the ship while the necessary repairs and maintenance were done.

One time while the ship was stopped, some sailors decided it was time to fish. One guy had a huge hook attached to a heavy rope he tied to the railing. He put a big hunk of bacon on the hook and threw it overboard. Instantly, the sea began to churn with giant fish as far as we could see. Someone exclaimed, "Those are sharks!" The sailor jerked sharply on the hook hoping to catch one, but the hook was empty.

It was amazing how quickly they came. Normally, there wasn't a shark in sight, but the moment the bacon was lowered, the sea seemed to boil with their thrashing. I think a person could have walked a mile on their backs without falling into the water. After several attempts and several pieces of lost bacon, the sailors gave up. I think the sharks were laughing.

We were free to explore the ship except for the bridge, the engine room, and the crew's quarters. The crew of course knew it was going to be really hot. To help with the heat, they mounted a large canvas roof toward the back of the ship – just ahead of the cannon. The tarp was tied to the railing and poles and created a nice shaded area on the deck. Before we knew it, a bunch of boys were on top of the canvas and there was much giggling and excitement and jumping around. I thought this looked like great fun and figured out how to grab the ropes, climb on the railing and pull myself up on top, too. It was like a trampoline, but there was nothing to hang onto and right at the edge far below was the sea.

I had about decided it was time to get down, when suddenly boys from below starting pushing upward and bouncing us. I flew into the air and on the way down I realized there was nothing to hang onto, and right below me was the foaming sea. Fortunately, I didn't panic. I looked around and saw one of the ropes holding the canvas. I grabbed the rope quickly and swung myself around and landed on the deck. Realizing how truly dangerous this was, that was the end of my trampoline adventures and I steered clear of the top of the canvas. Luckily, none of the other boys fell off the boat either, and to my knowledge we didn't lose a single person to the sea during our 28-day trip.

In general, the food on the ship tasted pretty good. It was different than we were used to, and there were more potatoes and not much rice. We ate in a big dining hall at long tables bolted to the floor. What I liked the best was Jell-O. I had never seen Jell-O before and it was pretty and jiggly, and tasted so sweet and good.

The Suez Canal

We arrived at the Suez Canal at Port Said and prepared to go through the canal. Only one ship at a time could go through parts of the canal so we had to wait our turn. To our surprise, we were suddenly herded off the ship and onto a train. Arrangements had been made by the Red Cross for all of us refugees to get warm clothing and supplies so we could handle Holland's colder weather. This necessary delay in going through the Suez Canal was determined to be the time to provide these items.

This was exciting, too, as I had never before been on a train, and I eagerly climbed aboard. My mother was still in the ship's hospital so it was just my father and Huibert and me. When we started moving I walked from wagon to wagon through the train to see what it was all about, and headed toward the end of the train. It moved fairly slowly so it was easy for me to walk through the cars. I wanted to get to the last car to see everything from the small platform peeking out from it. I finally made it to the last car, and opened the door with eager anticipation to enjoy the view. I was immediately hit smartly in the face with hot ashes and pieces of coal. These were spit out of the locomotive as the fire was stoked to make steam to drive the train.

I didn't realize there would be a down-draft caused by the moving train, so with cinders in my eyes, I knew I wouldn't be enjoying the view from the end of the train.

After a short ride, we came to a halt near a camp of enormous tents. We disembarked and the first thing we saw was a huge table loaded with sandwiches. There were buns filled with meats and cheeses and wonderful-smelling things. No one knew this food was for us and while our mouths were watering, we walked away not knowing what to do. Finally somebody said we could take the food, but we wondered where and how we should pay for it. At last, we discovered the food was free and for us, and we ate. Even then, it was not comfortable for us because we were not used to walking around eating. To us, eating was a sit-down situation.

Thinking about this, perhaps this memory was my first exposure to a "buffet," and this might be the reason I have never liked standing up eating at cocktail parties and that sort of thing. To this day, I don't like walking around a buffet to collect my food. To me, eating is still a sit-down situation.

After the sketchy meal, we were led to other tables covered with clothing. It was sort of like the army – someone looked at me and determined I would be a size whatever, and I was given some clothes. It went quickly and we were all outfitted for cold weather. Actually, they were very nice clothes and what I received was a pair of short pants, knickers ending just below the knee. The men were given long pants, but we kids got knickers. We got long socks to wear with them, and I really liked the shoes; good leather shoes that fit well. I was given a good cap and a scarf, and we all received the same warm winter coats that were brown. I'm sure we got underwear and shirts, too, but I remember the shoes best and I wore them for a long time.

Included in the huge tent, which was air conditioned, I was surprised to see a playground with swings and slides and things for the kids. There were several men there to help the little ones with the playground equipment. These men were very tall, tanned, blue-eyed Europeans, who somehow looked out of place with the English people who seemed to be running the whole enterprise. I found out later these were German prisoners of war who had apparently not yet been released after the war – men who had been under the command of the famous German General Erwin Rommel, known as the "Desert Fox[8]." What a come-down this must have been for these fierce Rommel fighters, to now be reduced to helping children get on and off the swings.

When the lunch and the clothing distribution were finished, we got back on the train and returned to the ship. During the wait to go through the canal, there were many small sailboats with Egyptian and Arab merchants eager to sell us things. These sailboats pulled up close to our ship and the merchants were shouting back and forth to people on the ship about their wares. They had purses and handbags, sandals and clothing and other things, and they were very aggressive about selling their wares.

The sailboats were way smaller than the ship and there was a great distance to the deck of the ship. The way they handled this distance was to have a young kid from the sailboat climb to the top of their mast. Even from there, he could barely look over the railing of the ship. He would cast a rope to the railing and they would then trade goods and money. Unfortunately, these weren't the most trustworthy sort of merchants, and when one of the crew from the

---

[8] From Wikipedia®: Rommel was a highly decorated officer in World War I. In World War II, he further distinguished himself as the commander of the 7th Panzer Division during the 1940 invasion of France. His leadership of German and Italian forces in the North African campaign established him as one of the most able commanders of the war. His campaign in North Africa earned Rommel the nickname the "Desert Fox" from British journalists. Rommel is regarded as having been a humane and professional officer. His "Afrika Korps" was never accused of war crimes, and soldiers captured during his Africa campaign were reported to have been treated humanely. Orders to kill Jewish soldiers, civilians and captured commandos were ignored. Late in the war, Rommel was linked to the conspiracy to assassinate Adolf Hitler, and arrested. Because Rommel was a national hero, Hitler desired to eliminate him quietly. He forced Rommel to commit suicide with a cyanide pill, in return for assurances that Rommel's family would not be persecuted following his death.

ship gave a large bill and expected change, he didn't get it. There was a lot of loud language back and forth and no change forthcoming, and the ship was about to leave. The yelling continued and the boy wanted them to untie the rope from the ship railing, and the crew member wouldn't do it. Suddenly, the ship began to move, dragging the boat. The sailboat was careening sideways so it even began to take water and we saw some of their goods go floating away. The next thing we saw was the kid climbing the mast again with a knife and this time he cut the rope. This made the sailboat immediately right itself, and the mast thrashed from side to side with the boy clinging for dear life. Watching the whiplash of the sailboat rocking back and forth and merchandise falling hither and thither into the canal was almost comical. To the merchants it appeared to be normal operating procedure and when the boat settled down, they calmly dived in the water to retrieve their goods. We went on through the canal and the Arabs sailed away to sell their wares to others.

A mean thing happened when one merchant sailboat came closer to the ship. A bunch of older boys from the ship had some boiled eggs which weren't all that fresh or hard-boiled. Everyone was hungry after the war and when the boys looked down and yelled to the local Arab guys on the boat if they wanted the eggs, they were eager to get any sort of food. The boys then threw the eggs as hard as they could and pelted the merchants, splattering bad-smelling egg parts in all directions. I was upset at the actions of the boys and felt sorry for the merchants, and I never had anything to do with any of those boys afterwards.

We made it through the Suez Canal and we were now in the Mediterranean Sea with a new view and new adventures.

Perils of the seas

There were many days when all we could see was water on all sides. It was an awesome experience to sight land after days at sea. It was always a happy occasion with people jumping around yelling,

"Land, land!" Sometimes what we thought was land would turn out to only be a cloud formation, but it was always exciting.

While we were moving, behind the ship was a trail of foam created by the propellers. We watched the foam to see if we varied from our course or made any turns, and this was especially something to look at while we were without sight of land for days at a time. The Indian Ocean was beautifully blue and the foam looked like whipped cream spread out behind the ship as far as we could see. In contrast, the waters of the Mediterranean were more brownish-colored, and the foam was pearly white.

While we were moving along in the Mediterranean at a pretty good clip, we saw another ship ahead of us going in the other direction. It was quite far away and I don't really know what sort of ship it was, but they were signing to our ship. We heard the flap flap flap of the signing equipment on our own bridge, and they were chattering back and forth with the lights and the flappers. All of a sudden we looked at the back of the ship and the foam in the wake was beginning to make a gigantic curve. For no reason we could see, the ship made a huge turn and then turned back to go straight again. Everyone was curious by this time, and someone finally sighted the reason for our change in course. There was a large mine floating in the water; one of those big round things with spikes sticking out all over. It was right in the path of our previous course and if we hadn't been warned by the oncoming ship, we could well have hit it and been blown right out of the water.

We had no more scary incidents in the Mediterranean and soon came to the Strait of Gibraltar at the southern tip of Spain. From there we went out into the Atlantic Ocean and on to the Bay of Biscay.

The Bay of Biscay is known for its storms and there is something unusual about the wave length in that area because of how the Bay is formed. For this reason, almost everyone who sails there gets seasick, and we were no exception. The waves were huge and terribly frightening, being the only real storms we saw on our whole voyage.

During daytimes, sick or not, we were on the deck, and hanging tightly onto whatever was handy.

One day, I looked up in shock at a wave that was many stories higher than our ship. In a flash we were on top of the wave, with our propeller out of the water and spinning around helplessly. Immediately, to my everlasting horror, we dived chaotically straight down into the valley created by the next monster wave.

The voyage comes to an end

With empty stomachs and whip-lashed bodies, we survived the Bay of Biscay. We went through the English Chanel without incident and were told we would arrive in Rotterdam the next morning, May 24, 1946. With 824 passengers aboard the ship, it was like traveling with a small city – one I was eager to leave behind as I embarked on the next chapter of my life's adventures.

Chapter 5

God, the Queen, and Holland

Aftermath of World War II in Holland

The Netherlands had maintained a policy of neutrality during World War I, and managed to remain outside the war while many of their neighbors fell to the Germans. The country tried again to remain neutral when World War II began, and they were assured by Hitler with a promise of nonaggression. Like other promises made by Hitler and the Nazis, it was a lie. On May 10, 1940, the German army began invasion of the Netherlands. After only five days of fighting, the Netherlands fell to the Germans, when they threatened to bomb the city of Rotterdam, the Netherland's major harbor. To add insult to injury, after the surrender, Rotterdam was bombed anyway, and the harbor significantly damaged.

At the end of World War II, besides opening its doors to thousands of refugees from their colony of the Dutch East Indies, Holland itself was reeling from the aftereffects of war. Many cities had been bombed, including Rotterdam, especially. Goods were scarce and everyone was struggling.

The Dutch famine of 1944, known in Dutch as the *Hongerwinter* (Hunger Winter), was a famine that took place in the German-occupied part of the Netherlands during the winter of 1944–1945. A German blockade cut off food and fuel shipments from farm areas.

Some 4.5 million people were affected and more than 20,000 died directly because of starvation or cold. Most vulnerable according to death reports were elderly men.

There was a strategic action called "Operation Market Garden" toward the end of the war led by British Field Marshal Bernard Montgomery. This was supposed to gain control of the bridge across the Rhine River at Arnhem, and subsequently take control of German industrial areas. Waves of paratroopers were not supported by enough ground troops and the operation failed. The Germans then put an embargo on food and fuel supplies going to the western Netherlands. The embargo, along with an unusually harsh winter caused untold suffering to an already war-weakened population.

The failure of the Market Garden ruined Allied hopes to end the war by Christmas 1944. The embargo was partially lifted in early November 1944, allowing some food transports over water, but an early and abnormally cold winter caused the canals to freeze over and barges could not deliver their precious cargo.

In May 1945, Operation Manna by the Royal Air Force and Royal Canadian Air Force, and Operation Chowhound, by the U.S. Air Force, dropped more than 11,000 tons of food into the western part of Holland to help feed starving civilians. After these life-saving efforts, Wikipedia® shows a faded photograph taken from the air of the words "Many Thanks" written in tulips by grateful farmers.

In light of the suffering by so many in the mother country, there had to be resentment for refugees streaming from the Dutch East Indies, including my own family. I never experienced any outward display of bitterness at our being there. I suspect my parents did, but they never spoke of it.

I know the Dutch were firm in safeguarding their communities from what they perceived as misconduct by their own citizens. There were people in Holland who were collaborators with the Germans and they were arrested and put in camps. There were also women who had had close relations with the Germans, and they were picked up and their heads were shaved as a punishment. I never saw any of these bald-headed women, but I heard about them. I don't know whether these women were forced to have relations with the Germans as so called "comfort women," or did so willingly. Whatever the case, they suffered the embarrassment of shaved heads for a short time, and the mental anguish of the horrors that might have been done to them, for the rest of their lives.

During the war, the Germans had put land mines in the sand dunes that edged the sea. In case of invasion by Allied forces from the sea, they fortified the coastline from Norway and Denmark, Holland and Belgium, all the way down through France. They peppered the dunes with land mines all along the coast, including near Zandvoort, where my family lived.

Most of the dunes around Zandvoort were swept clean, but by no means were they able to find every mine. Some areas had barbed wire surrounding the dunes, with serious "No Trespassing, Mine Field" signs posted. What they had done and were still doing while I was there, was using German prisoners of war and Dutch collaborators, giving them a map and telling them to clean up the mine fields. After the mines were cleared, they made the prisoners walk hand in hand back and forth over the area to be sure all of the mines were gone. I can imagine knowing what they would have to do afterwards, they did a good job of cleaning up the mines. I never heard of any mishap of finding a forgotten mine in the Zandvoort dunes.

Arriving in Rotterdam

Our excitement was beyond description when we actually reached Holland. Growing up in Indonesia, we learned from the cradle on, the Queen of Holland was second only to God. Holland was a fantasy land and basically the capital of the world, where everything was perfect. Through my entire education the Dutch people had served as models for conduct and comportment. Our expectations were massive and I dreamed of seeing everyone in wooden shoes and blond hair. All girls wore their hair in braids, all women wore aprons, and men were strong. I could hardly wait to see these beautiful people.

Reality set in as we pulled slowly into the harbor early in the morning. Men were pulling the ship to the dock with huge ropes and walking back and forth. It was the end of May and still kind of chilly out so they were wearing jackets. I looked at their feet and they wore low leather boots instead of wooden shoes. I called out in amazement, "Look at their feet – they're wearing *shoes!*" I was shocked and disappointed.

This shock must have blocked my other memories because I don't remember disembarking the ship with Huibert and my father. My mother was moved directly from the ship to the hospital in Rotterdam, so we didn't even see her for a couple of weeks.

We were loaded on a large touring bus along with a lot of other people from the ship and our meager luggage. I knew the terrain in Holland would be flat, but it was flatter than flat. As we rode along, the flatness made me miss the mountains and palm trees from my home in Indonesia, so it was with mixed emotions that I looked around me at the beauty of this foreign land I had learned so much about.

It was nice weather and we could see for miles. Families were dropped off at hotels and homes and villas, and we drove through a beautiful part of Holland as we crisscrossed through the primary tulip fields. Unknown to me, it was the height of the tulip season. It was like riding on carpets of yellow and red, more beautiful than I could ever have imagined. Even more important, I began to see people wearing wooden shoes as they tended to the tulips. Finally, I felt like I had truly arrived in the Holland of my dreams.

We were the last people on the bus when we got to our destination in Zandvoort, southwest of Amsterdam on the banks of the North Sea. This gave us the chance to see many areas of the country and many different types of homes where people were dropped off. Some of these houses were large mansions which had been confiscated by the Germans during the war and later converted by the Dutch as multiple family dwellings for refugees.

One stop before we got to Zandvoort, the bus driver was looking for an address he couldn't find. He saw a boy walking and he stopped to ask for directions. The boy said, "Oh, I'll bring you there!" The boy climbed on the bus and took us exactly where we wanted to go. The boy was the epitome of what I thought of as a Dutch boy, smiling and helpful and outgoing, and he even wore wooden shoes. The others must have thought so, too, because he got many admiring glances from the women.

Home away from home

We arrived in the village of Zandvoort at Hogeweg 56 (Highroad 56) which was Tante Fie and Oom Anton's small hotel. Oom Anton was the younger brother of my grandfather van Demmeltraadt, but we had never before seen him.

My father got out and walked the small footpath to the door and rang the bell. Out of the door came the personification of what I considered to be a Dutch woman. Tante Fie was round and big-busted, with a round face and blond braids wound around her head, blue eyes and red cheeks. She immediately pressed Pa to her ample bosom and gave him a big kiss on each cheek. Huibert and I got the same treatment.

We started to go back to the bus for the luggage when Tante Fie said, "No, I'll send the help – his name is Gijs." This immediately took me back to when I learned to read in the Dutch East Indies. We had a wooden board with loose letters we had to fit on the board and there were pictures of people. One of the pictures was a boy named Gijs (pronounced Hice), and he was the help, or hired man. Of course, that was how I expected the "help" to look, and I wasn't disappointed. Gijs was dressed exactly as the boy in my picture: knickers and working boots, with leather "caps," (shin guards) and of course he was blond and blue-eyed.

Oom Anton apparently looked very much like my grandfather, so Pa must have been pleasantly surprised when he saw him. He, too, had never seen anyone else from his father's family. Oom Anton had been a bachelor and Tante Fie was married before and she became a widow, but had no children. Tante Fie owned another small hotel just a few buildings away from Oom Anton's building.

Anton had always been in the food service business. When he was quite young, he had a trailer he hauled around to fairgrounds and markets and town squares. He sold food out of the trailer – meatballs and French fries (called *patat friet*) and other types of food. People there ate French fries with mayonnaise or mustard (mayonnaise cost an extra five cents and was only for the big spenders). He was quite successful, but he had some scrapes with the law now and then, for parking his trailer in the wrong place. Anton was always known for using only the very best foods and ingredients, and he knew how to cook them, too.

Later on, Anton became the chef on board a Dutch freighter that went all over the world. He would be at sea for many months before going back to the ship's base, as the ship would pick up freight and haul to one point, get something else loaded and go to another point. There was no set route. He went to places like Amsterdam, Jakarta, New York, and all points between.

Eventually, he decided to settle in Zandvoort, and he bought a small family hotel in the charming village on the shores of the North Sea. His business was mainly in the summertime when guests would come from Amsterdam and Haarlem and other cities for "the season," to frolic on the seashore nearby. When Tante Fie became a widow, they met and married, then rented out the building she owned with her first husband, and came to live in Anton's hotel. They lived in a small apartment in the basement of the hotel, which had an open walk-out entrance in the back.

We arrived in Zandvoort about two weeks before the season began in mid-June. We were able to stay in the main hotel for those two weeks, but when guests arrived, we moved to the basement to share Oom Anton and Tante Fie's apartment. They had one bedroom, our family of four had the other, and there was a small living/dining area, plus the large kitchen where all food for the hotel was prepared. One good thing was they also had a big bathroom in the basement for all our family to use, plus the two of them, and it even had a bathtub with a hand shower, which I discovered was rare.

The hotel had about 20 guest rooms of various sizes, with some suites and some small rooms. Of course there were no radios or televisions in hotel rooms at that time. There was a pay phone in the hall, and there were no bathrooms, which was customary. Each bedroom in the hotel had only a small sink. At the end of the hall on each floor was a toilet. One toilet for each floor, and no shower or bathtub. All of the smaller hotels were like this in Holland. Thinking about this now, I can't imagine how tough it was for the guests to clean up after spending the whole day by the sea, with wind and sand and all.

The practice in those days was to go to a public bathhouse to bathe, and each village had one bathhouse, and only one. Each person took their own towel and soap, and hopefully clean clothes, and went to the bathhouse once a week to bathe or shower.

This was appalling to my family, and I expect to all Indos who came to Holland. We came from the Dutch East Indies where everyone, rich, poor, or otherwise, bathed or showered daily, and usually twice daily. Cleanliness was something deeply ingrained in me. I couldn't believe there were people who only washed once a week. In addition to not washing their bodies properly, we learned they didn't wash their behinds either. At the risk of sounding coarse, it has always been customary for Indos to use a bottle of water to wash after using the toilet, with paper only for drying off.

After frantically looking for the "bottle" after using the toilet in the hotel, I found there was only paper, and no water for washing. This was "the last straw," and to be honest, it changed my view of the Dutch at that time. Fortunately, times have changed through the years, and everyone has full bathrooms now, and uses them appropriately. However, I would be willing to wager that every Indo home to this day still has bottles of water beside their commodes.

My mother comes back

After a couple of weeks in the hospital in Rotterdam, my father went to get my mother to bring her to our hotel home. She was weak after being ill for so long, but able to take the train. The station was not far from Oom Anton's hotel, and they were able to walk from there. My mother did well in the healthy sea air in Zandvoort, as there were likely fewer allergens in the air. In those days, people didn't know as much about the causes of asthma, and that allergies were such a significant factor. When we later moved to The Hague, farther inland and a much larger city, she began to again have problems and spent time in the hospital in Scheveningen nearby.

Daily life in Zandvoort

I don't know what my mother did with her time while we were with Oom Anton and Tante Fie. She was still not well, so maybe she didn't have duties. I know Pa helped Oom Anton around the hotel with maintenance. There always seemed to be something needing fixing, like metal beds that fell apart, and leaky plumbing and the like. Pa wasn't too well either, having recently come from a prison camp where he was starved and often sick with malaria and other ailments. He helped as much as he could.

Trip to the zoo

One day we took a trip to the zoo in Amsterdam. A friend of Huibert's went with us on the light rail train and it was quite an outing. I see in the picture I was wearing my new knickers and sturdy shoes I received while crossing the Suez Canal. My mother was with us also, and she must have taken the picture. Sad to say, I don't have a single photograph of the four of us together either in Holland or Indonesia. Whether none were ever taken or they were lost along the way is a sad mystery.

Figure 12 Huibert and me with our father at the zoo in Amsterdam in 1946. A friend of Huibert's is on the left. Photo taken by Erna van Demmeltraadt, deceased.

The Amsterdam zoo was much larger than the one we knew in Bandung, but for some reason it was not as exciting for me. What was exciting about our trips to the Bandung zoo before the war was the enormous elephant there. Even more exciting was the memory of my believing the elephant danced on my command. There was also an orangutan which once shook Pa's hand. The thrilling sight of that strong grip between man and beast will remain with me always.

Back to school

All of us from the Dutch East Indies had had a forced vacation of four years from school, because the Japanese closed all of the Dutch-language-based schools during their occupation. The only school available during the war was a specific Indonesian school in an unreachable place and the only language spoken there was Bahasa.

Bahasa was a recently made-up language which was eventually considered the "official" Indonesian language after they achieved their independence. We did not speak Bahasa (most people didn't) but in addition to Dutch, we spoke the more common language which everyone was able to speak, loosely called "the market language."

Overall, according to our age, we were way behind in normal schooling. The Dutch arranged a special school in Haarlem, about 10 miles from Zandvoort, for refugee children, and classes were designed to push us through two years of schooling in one. They called them "bridge" classes, to build a bridge from where we had stopped our schooling because of the war, to where we should be in our classes.

In all, I went through four years of schooling in the two years we were in Holland. We focused on reading, writing, mathematics, geography, and history. There were no music or sports classes or anything considered extraneous to basic learning. School was not hard for me and I enjoyed my classes.

Each day Huibert and I walked a couple of blocks and boarded the light rail train for our trip to Haarlem, which took probably a half-hour. There was no lunch room in the school, so we took a simple lunch of bread and cheese from home each day. The school was about four blocks from the station, and we were careful to always be on time so as not to miss our train home.

It was stimulating for us to be in Holland – everything was new. The streets were narrow and everything seemed small to us, and it was all so very different from what we knew. We didn't mingle much with the local boys. There were a few Indo boys in Zandvoort who became friends, but for some reason it seemed to be a mutual decision to not become friends with the local boys.

The weather in Holland was cold for all of us who were used to a hot tropical climate, and as we huddled in our school room, some of the other kids began to smell more rank than the Dutch. Many of the boys came to school with their pajamas peeking out from under their shirts, and I expect they crawled out of bed and put their clothes on right over their pajamas. It was just too cold to be naked and wet besides, and cleanliness suffered.

Figure 13 My school class in Haarlem, 1946. We Indo children were taught separately from the Dutch kids, because we had a lot of catching up to do. There were no classes in Indonesia during the war, so from age 7 to 11, I had no schooling at all. (I'm in the middle left of the photo holding up my ruler in my left hand.) Photographer unknown.

My first winter

In the late fall, there were fierce storms I had never before experienced. In Zandvoort by the sea the winds howled and whipped the sea into a state of frenzy, with huge waves. Always curious about new adventures, I was not afraid and loved to walk in the wind, feeling exhilarated by its force. This was a totally new encounter for me and I reluctantly retreated to the house which was cozy and warm with hurricane-force winds whirling outside.

When winter came, it was especially thrilling to Huibert and me. We greeted the cold and the snow and the ice as remarkable new inventions made especially for our entertainment. Every day was a new adventure.

Oom Anton and Tante Fie could see our delight and made the winter special for us. They got the house ready for Santa Claus (*Sinterklaas*) to come on December 5. The story of *Sinterklaas* is that a Spanish bishop who came from a well-to-do family centuries before, went to poor neighborhoods and brought gifts, most likely things to eat. Holland was occupied by Spain in the Middle Ages, so that's probably where the tradition came from. Practically all of Europe still celebrates Saint Nicholas' Eve on December 4. Many times the gifts are like what we now call gag-gifts – small things which could be funny, although it was usually some form of food. In contrast, Christmas is a serious and religious time and gifts are more serious then, too. Saint Nicholas' Eve is more fun. From *Sinterklaas* that year I got a chocolate "O," which is a very common Dutch gift – the first letter of your name, in chocolate. Later, for Christmas that year, I got a fountain pen.

At Christmas, we had a real tree that was decorated with real candles and all kinds of beautiful decorations on it. And, of course, Tante Fie did the baking. All of her best things came out at Christmas.

When we were young, in Bandung, the night before *Sinterklaas* came, we put a carrot in our shoe beside our bed and some hay for his white horse, plus a glass of water for *Sinterklaas*. In the morning we usually had something in our shoe – a chocolate letter or some little gift. Black Pete was the one who carried *Sinterklaas'* bag of treats. (Black Pete, or *Zwarte Piet*, is the servant of *Sinterklaas*. Some say he got his name because he carried the gifts down the chimneys and his face was black from soot. Others say he was a Moor, a dark-skinned man from Spain or North Africa. The mythical fellow has become a controversial character and continues to draw negative attention from commentators and news organizations around the world. He remains a popular character in the Dutch culture.)

We lived in fear of *Zwarte Piet* because he carried a switch (a bunch of spines of large palm branches with the leaves taken off, which was used by natives to beat rugs) and he would use it to whip naughty children. The legend said when his bag of treats was empty, he would grab naughty children and put them in his bag. One Saint Nicholas' evening back in Indonesia, I saw someone waving a palm branch outside our window. I was so terrified, I ran as fast as I could and leaped into Pa's lap. I felt protected and knew Pa would save me from *Zwarte Piet*.

In Holland, snuggly tucked into Oom Anton and Tante Fie's hotel, we eagerly waited for the snow we had heard so much about. When it finally came, it was a breathtaking sight – the white flakes falling gently to the ground all around us. We didn't even feel the cold because of our excitement at seeing this wonderful new phenomenon. We raced outside, even dragging Tante Fie, and immediately had a snowball fight, all of us peppering each other with snowballs and laughing all the while.

About half a block away was a car dealership and repair shop, and they had a big square where they might have parked cars at one time. It was nice and level and made of cement squares. In the winter they flooded and froze this square so the village people would have a place to skate at a small price. My father had always been a good roller-skater and could do fancy-antsy stuff on roller skates. Before the ice was fully frozen on the square there was Pa wearing a pair of figure skates, and he quickly learned how to skate rings around us boys.

Huibert and I had the common Dutch skates, a wooden frame with an iron blade embedded in it, and they were strapped onto our shoes. We had also done some roller skating in Indonesia, so it was just a matter of getting used to the blade. In no time at all we were skating around the ice like we'd done it all our lives. For Huibert these skates weren't fast enough, so he got some racing skates, boots with long blades and he really liked going around and around as fast as he could.

Rationing

When we arrived in 1946, food and other items were rationed. Each family was allowed only so much flour, sugar, meat, butter, cheese, and other items. We had to have coupons from the government to get almost anything we needed.

We refugees were allowed more coupons than others, double, I think. This did not sit well with the Dutch folks, but we got them anyway. We gave all of our coupons to Oom Anton and Tante Fie, because they did the cooking and provided all of our food. Also, because of the hotel, they got extra coupons, too. So Oom Anton, master chef that he was, was able to get all of the first class meats and foods with which he preferred to cook; no shortcuts for him. In fact, he prepared healthy gourmet meals three times a day. Everything he cooked was superb, and his baking was out of this world. I still remember the taste of his apple pies as the best I have ever had in my life. And his steaks were wonderful and his *shu*, or sauce, and his Brussel sprouts. I could go on and on.

Our family ate earlier than Oom Anton and Tante Fie. I must have been a very slow eater then as I am now, and many times I would still be at the table alone when they came to eat. This was after the maids had served us and the work was finished, and then Oom Anton and Tante Fie sat down and the maids served them. Tante Fie would say to me, "Oh, Onno, have some more of this, and how about some of that ..." and I would end up eating a whole second meal. I was happy to do it because the food was so delicious.

Tante Fie was just as good a cook as her husband, but Oom Anton didn't think so sometimes. During the season, when the guests were there from mid-June until September, Oom Anton did the cooking. On the last day, when the guests left, he would clean up the kitchen and turn it over to Tante Fie, who cooked the rest of the year. Unfortunately, she was known for using shortcuts on occasion. For example, one evening Tante Fie did something in a hurry with the *shu*. Oom Anton filled his plate with meat, potatoes, and something else. He lifted the bowl with the gravy, looked at it, and said, "I don't need this," and shoved the bowl away. She protested, but he got up and said, "I'm done eating," and walked away. No one else could tell any difference in the gravy, but something was different and he wouldn't touch it until she corrected her "shortcut" and made a whole new bowl of *shu*.

Another example of Oom Anton's rigid tastes was when he was persuaded by Tante Fie to go out to eat one evening. This was something he just didn't want to do, but for years Tante Fie had been pestering him to go out for something at one of the other well-known restaurants. He finally relented and agreed to go to a first class restaurant in the larger city of Haarlem. They had heard about the restaurant and he hoped it would be worth an evening away.

They got to the restaurant where he hung his hat and coat and they were shown to a fine table, and they ordered. Anton ordered a special cut of meat known to be the finest available, which was a special feature of this restaurant. It might have been some sort of top sirloin or the like. Finally, the waiter came with the food, beautifully presented on a fine china plate which had been heated to enhance the flavors, and set it before Anton.

He took one look at the meat, and said, "Oh waiter, I thought I ordered the special cut."

The waiter said, "Oh yes, sir. This is what you ordered."

"No it's not. I ordered the special cut. I don't know what this is, but it's not the special cut."

"Oh yes, sir, it is, it is exactly what you ordered."

Anton said, "You can take it back, it's not what I ordered."

The waiter left and came back with the plate and said the cook verified this was the special cut of meat. When Anton refused to eat it, the waiter said, "Well what am I to do with it?"

Anton stood up and said with a haughty air, "Well, you can rub it in your hair, or you can use it to polish your shoes, whatever you like. Come Fie, we're finished here."

With that, he donned his coat and hat, grabbed his wife who was still sitting there looking longingly at her plate, and marched out of the restaurant.

This was the first and last "eating out" event for Tante Fie and Oom Anton.

The shot

My father was stricken with malaria as were most of the POWs on Sumatra. I witnessed him succumbing to two attacks of malaria, one in Jakarta and one after we got to Holland, and neither was a pretty sight.

Officially, he was still in the army because the soldiers were required to return to Holland to be discharged. Before he got discharged not long after we arrived in Zandvoort, he did get treated by a doctor from the army who was also originally from Indonesia. The doctor said there was no way to get rid of the malaria and Pa would have unexpected attacks for the rest of his life, as thousands of others did. My father was insistent if he had to live with malaria, he would rather not live at all, and he was willing to do anything to be rid of it.

The doctor told him there was an extremely experimental treatment he could give him – one exceedingly potent and formidable shot. However, the shot was so powerful there was a 50-50 chance of death when it was administered. In fact, the doctor told him if he survived the shot with 50-50 odds, there was only a slim chance he would be rid of the malaria and not be bothered by future attacks.

They determined my father had a strong heart, and was healthy otherwise. Since he was so resolute about not living with malaria, they decided to give him the shot. Not only did he did get the shot, he survived. After the shot, he did have one more attack of malaria, which might have actually been after-effects of the shot, but after that event, to my knowledge, he never again had any major problems with malaria. My father died at age 74 in Houston, Texas of something unrelated to malaria.

My father's discharge from the Army

Not long after he received the critical malaria shot, my father was honorably discharged from Her Majesty's Royal Dutch East Indies Army. There were no parades, no fanfare; he simply came home to Zandvoort.

I have recently been in contact with a man in Oregon, Wes Injerd, who I mentioned earlier has continued the extensive work of Roger Mansell, the founder of the Center for Research, Allied POWs Under the Japanese. Injerd sent me by email my father's POW Index Card, something no one in our family knew existed until now. Written in Japanese and Dutch, the card shows F.E.M. van Demmeltraadt's capture in Java on March 8, 1942, and other information including his parents' names, and his occupation, listed as "automobile repairman." The reverse side of the card shows the POW camps where my father was imprisoned. While the information is minimal, it answers some of our questions as to where he spent the war. I am most grateful to have it.

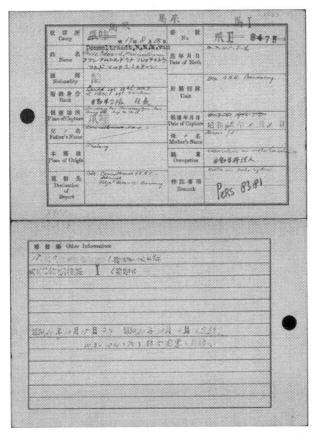

Figure 14 Frits van Demmeltraadt's POW Index Card. Provided by Wes Injerd. Public domain.

Pa returns to Indonesia

My father did not find real work in Holland. He had been looking and talking with auto and motorcycle dealers in the area for many months. In Haarlem there was a man who was a noted motor racer and he raced on a BMW motorcycle. Pa went there to talk with him, but the man's business was only for one person and he didn't need help.

An additional problem to finding work and blending in with the Dutch community was the sad fact that Indos were not well accepted by the Dutch people. There was resentment because of costs involved in feeding thousands of extra people when resources were in short supply for everyone, plus bitterness because people they saw as interlopers were taking jobs they felt should have gone to pure Dutch folks.

After a year, my father was in better health and eager to find work, but there were simply no opportunities in his field. He was discouraged by the resentments felt by the Dutch, and he wasn't happy with the climate in Holland overall. He decided to return to Indonesia to see if he could find some business opportunities there.

When my father left to return to Bandung where his brother Joop still lived, my mother and Huibert and I moved to The Hague. This was a major city in Holland closer to Amsterdam, and the government center for the Netherlands. It is also where a large number of Indos had settled. We lived there with my mother's half-sister Tante Mien, and her family. Her children were Ina, Hanna, and Peter, and her husband was Oom Guus, who was a Dutch Reform Protestant pastor. However, even though Oom Guus had a large church and congregation in Indonesia, his ministerial license was not recognized in Holland. He was only able to assist in churches of other pastors for a long time. Eventually he formed his own church of primarily Indo parishioners, and was a successful pastor for many years.

Tante Mien's house in The Hague was owned by the sister of Karel Doorman, the Dutch admiral who fought against the Japanese during the war. Tante Mien's daughters Ina and Hanna were grown and working when we lived there, but they lived with their parents. Ina was working for the Royal Dutch airline and eventually married and moved to the U.S. Hanna later married another Dutch minister and they moved to the West Indies, to Surinam.

I never enjoyed living in The Hague. I was used to the room and space and freedom we had in Zandvoort, and I felt confined in The Hague because of its large and concentrated population. Huibert was happier there because he had discovered girls, and there was an abundance of them, but circumstances changed. About a year after he left, my father was able to reestablish himself in business in Indonesia and he sent for his family to join him.

Figure 15 A precious picture of my mother and me, taken in early 1948 while we lived in The Hague. Photo taken by Frits van Demmeltraadt, deceased.

I was thrilled to return to my beloved homeland and willingly helped to load our scanty belongings on another ship for the trip. This time, we sailed on a real passenger ship, the *Johan van Oldenbarneveldt*. Instead of jolting along in the freighter as we had on our trip to Holland, we had comfortable accommodations, real dining rooms with wonderful food, and even a swimming pool. It was like a vacation and the best part was that we were going home.

Chapter 6

Return to Indonesia

Indonesia's struggle for independence

We arrived in Jakarta in late spring of 1948. Indonesia had not yet established its independence after declaring it in August 1945. The political situation was still volatile, but not as bad as during the full blast of the Bersiap from 1945 to early 1948. The Allied forces, using mainly British troops, had gained control of the cities and driven the rebels to the outer-lying areas. Also, Holland had begun to reestablish its army so they were again a presence in the country and had secured the main roads of some cities. Sukarno and his troops were still stirring up trouble with the natives, but they were primarily located around the city of Jogjakarta in Central Java.

We continued to believe that Holland would reestablish its authority over the country and life would continue much as it had before the war. While this was a naive approach to the precarious position of a post-war country seeking its own independence, I can only say it was the way my own family thought, and it was the belief of many others at the time, also.

Popular beliefs aside, Indonesia secured its independence on November 2, 1949. The following information from *History Today*,[9] states:

---

[9] *History Today* Volume: 49, Issue 11 1999. Permission received from Dean Nicholas, Website manager, *History Today*.

Equipped with Japanese weapons, the nationalists waged an armed struggle against the Dutch, who had powerful economic reasons for recovering the East Indies and also believed that most Indonesians wanted them to return. Dutch forces made substantial headway in Java and Sumatra, but there was fierce criticism in the United Nations, and the United States pressed for a negotiated solution. Eventually a conference of 120 delegates assembled at The Hague in August 1949 under the chairmanship of the Dutch Prime Minister, Willem Drees. The nationalist delegates were skillfully led by Hatta. On November 2nd, after ten weeks of haggling, the conference reached an agreement which transferred Dutch sovereignty to the United States of Indonesia, with Queen Juliana of the Netherlands as titular head of a new Netherlands-Indonesian Union, Sukarno as Indonesian President, and Mohammad Hatta as Prime Minister.

Perilous trip from Jakarta

My father was jubilantly awaiting our ship's arrival in Jakarta. Eager to get his family home, we drove the three-hour trip to Bandung by car, about 110 miles, on a curvy road that goes up and down a mountain range and into the valley where Bandung rests. There was an area close to Bandung where rebels were known to be hiding in the hills and ambushes could take place. In addition to native rebels, there were a number of former Japanese soldiers who never surrendered after the war and became renegades. These insurgents lived in the mountains and often attacked and robbed people on the smaller roads around cities. In fact, not long after we returned to Indonesia a business associate of my father was attacked on a lonely stretch of road, and murdered by a group of renegades.

When we got to the dangerous point in the road, my father slowed down and took out his pistol, which he kept under the seat. He always kept his pistol at the ready in case of trouble, particularly on that road. Fortunately, we were not ambushed that day, or on other trips on that road for the rest of our life in Indonesia. I've wondered later how effective that one little pistol would have been against the larger weapons of ambushing rebels.

Returning to life in Bandung

Happily arriving in our home town, we first took quarters with my father's brother Joop and his family, moving in with the five of them. It was toward the end of the school year there. We had just come from Holland, where we took four years of classes in two years because of having no school in Indonesia during the Japanese occupation. I had missed many classes, but more or less, I went to school with my age-level group.

We stayed several months with Oom Joop's family while my father established his business. Before long, the business bought a house outside the city. It was a nice big house and we moved there along with Jan Bartels, Pa's business partner, who was single at the time. The name of the area where the house was built was called "*Dennelust*," which loosely translates, "pine tree delight." It was a lush neighborhood with many beautiful pine trees, large houses with lovely yards, and built part way up the mountain. Soon after we moved there, we discovered less than a block away lived Pa's friend, J. J. J. de Jong, the man who flew us to Jakarta after the war.

Our home was a spacious two-story house, with a triple garage, kitchen and outbuildings in the back where the *kokkie* (cook) stayed with her husband. The rooms behind the garage were equipped with their own separate conveniences, including a bathroom with a squatting toilet that the natives preferred rather than the high toilets in the WCs (water closets) in the rest of the house. There was also a "*put*" in the back, an open well which was used for laundry water, while the rest of the house had full plumbing with city water piped in. There were two stairways leading to the second floor; a wooden staircase indoors, and a second of stone and tiles outside.

This house was in the same general area but several miles closer to the city than the beautiful house my father built before the war. That house and all its contents were lost to us because of the war.

Jan Bartels was a single man, quite a bit younger than Pa. He moved in with us and he had two dogs, a cocker spaniel and a mutt. Both were nice dogs and they were my friends. Being far from town and school, it wasn't easy for me to make friends with other boys, so I played mainly with the dogs. I think my favorite was the mongrel dog. He was a fast runner and I often took him along later when I rode my motorcycle around the neighborhood.

I rode to school with Pa and Jan when they went to work in the early morning. The school day ended at one o'clock when the men went home for lunch, so I rode home with them also. They had their big meal and then returned to work and I stayed home. I finished the sixth grade and fortunately passed the exam which allowed me to go to high school. I first went to high school at a private Dutch school called BSV which stood for Bandung School Association. This was the group of Dutch language schools that included the grade school Huibert and I attended before the war.

After Indonesian independence was achieved, the Indonesian government eventually closed the BSV and allowed only one Dutch-speaking Christian high school in Bandung, which was the Lyceum. I had secretly wanted all along to go to this school, and I transferred to the Lyceum in 1951 for my last two years of high school. I liked the overall atmosphere of this school and I made many friends there. My friend Bonthy Kiliaan also went to the Lyceum and we renewed our childhood friendship there.

There was an active student club at the Lyceum called *Vedo* (*Voor en Door Ons*, meaning For and By Us), which to this day remains a committed and operational group. In fact, *Vedo* organized the amazing all-school reunion in 2005, which my wife Gloria and I attended in Bandung along with more than 100 classmates. We currently have a large email group through Vedo which shares pictures and stories about students and families, and it is a source of much enjoyment for all of us.

A sad crash

When Japan surrendered, the occupational forces in Indonesia were British, with many soldiers from India and Pakistan. We Indos were disappointed because we had hoped the Americans would have liberated us. There was a sort of mystique about the Americans overall, and anything connected to them was exciting.

Holland began to again build up the Dutch East Indian Army. Many of the former military prisoners of war were still in the military as my father was before he went to Holland for treatment for malaria and his eventual discharge. One of the additions to the Dutch Air Force was a number of American planes, small one-pilot fighters known as Mustangs that routinely flew over Bandung on unknown missions. We young boys were keenly attuned to hearing the distinctive sound of the Mustang engines when the fighters were in the air and we loved to watch their endless climbs and scary swooping dives. Even in class, we listened for them when they flew over our school.

One day at school, in about mid-1949 when we were outside on our morning break, we heard a Mustang go high in the air and plunge toward the earth in what was a stunt-flying ear-shattering dive. As one, we waited with baited breath for the plane to pull out of its dive. Suddenly the screaming sound stopped abruptly. The silence was like a brutal slap on each of our faces. Again, as one, we ran out of the schoolyard to our bicycles, heedless of any rules or teachers in the way. We pedaled as fast as we could in the direction of the previous sound, terrified of what we would find, and yet knowing all the while it would not be good.

Our fears were realized – the plane had crashed in the middle of a popular restaurant nearby. It fell cleanly through the roof directly into the kitchen. Amazingly, no one was hurt in the restaurant, or the kitchen. It was just before lunchtime with few people around, and those who were there were probably outside watching the plane's screaming descent and able to get away.

Later, we heard the pilot's remains were found beneath the kitchen and wrapped around the engine of the plane. We never heard what happened or caused the crash, but I know none of us will ever forget the horrendous sound of the silence we heard that day.

My father's business

My father had some sort of business connection with a man named Meeuwenoord, one of the owners of the Chevrolet dealership in Bandung. I believe Pa might have borrowed money from him at one time, perhaps as a short-term loan before getting money from the bank to import motorcycles. He possibly also consulted with Meeuwenoord for business advice.

This relationship was renewed after the war, when nothing happened with business opportunities for Pa in Holland, and he returned to Indonesia. He was able to start up his motorcycle business again in the same building where we lived before the war. Little by little, he renewed alliances with motorcycle producers BMW, Harley Davidson, and Triumph.

Also, Pa and Meeuwenoord made a business deal which allowed my father to buy into the Chevrolet business along with Jan Bartels, who was a sort of foster child of Meeuwenoord. Jan's parents were running a sugar plantation way up in the mountains. In order for Jan to go to school, he stayed with Meeuwenoord and his wife for several years, and became very close to them. In fact, when the war started in Indonesia, Meeuwenoord told Jan he was welcome to go with him and his wife to Australia as he thought things were not going well in Indonesia. Jan chose to stay and join the army. Being full Dutch, Jan finished the war as a POW along with thousands of others, but stayed in Indonesia afterwards. Meeuwenoord returned to Bandung and likely through his connections, my father was able to start the Chevrolet dealership with Jan as his partner.

I believe Meeuwenoord approached Pa to somehow possibly step into the Chevrolet dealership business because Meeuwenoord had his eyes on bigger business ventures. This had to do with aircraft and flying, so even though his name and another partner by the name of Rous were on the building, my father and Jan Bartels were the principal owners. Pa and Jan built a successful business with the Chevrolet dealership. There were cars, but mainly pickups and trucks built in the U.S. and assembled in a GM factory in Jakarta.

Figure 16 The Chevrolet dealership and service station in Bandung owned and operated by Frits van Demmeltraadt and Jan Bartels. The name of the business was Dembar, from Demmeltraadt and Bartels. Photo by Jan Bartels, and used with his permission.

The service part of the business was busy as parts were difficult to get and everything was repaired rather than replaced. I visited the paint department of the service station one time and watched one of the native men paint a repaired design on a car fender. The man was nothing less than an artist as everything had to be done by hand. He mixed the color with his brush until it was just right, and then he looked at the fender, and looked at the fender for the longest time. I thought he was never going to do anything, when suddenly, he took the brush and swirled it along the edge of the fender in one quick smooth motion. The design was absolutely perfect. You couldn't tell any difference whatsoever from the other fender which had been done by a machine in an American factory.

Back to motorcycle racing

When my father came back to Indonesia, he was still remembered as the famous "Java Champion," but he only raced once after returning. The race was in Jakarta and he wanted to make a name for the brand of motorcycle he was selling. It was called a Jawa, a Czechoslovakian machine for which he had the distributorship. I believe he was also trying to impress the Dutch army, perhaps hoping to get more business from them.

The motorcycle was a two-cycle engine and it was very quiet. Initially, the motorcycle started fast and went like crazy, but the top speed wasn't there. Several Dutch soldiers raced also and I was watching the race near some other soldiers. One of them said, "What sort of machine is that? It's so quiet, it must run on sewing machine oil!"

Other cycles were soon passing him up because the Jawa just didn't have the speed, but my father was such a good rider, he could maneuver his machine better on the curves and was almost in the lead. Another racer, an old competitor from years before, was also in the race and he was determined to beat Pa. His machine was actually faster, but he wasn't the best rider, and while he passed my father up on the straight-away, he fell back on the curves. On one of the sharpest curves, the competitor, in a foolish move, tried to pass Pa on the inside, thinking he could intimidate him. This was not only dangerous, but foolhardy. My hard-headed father refused to yield and the competitor slid into him, sending them both flying over the dirt. We saw dust flying and heard the abrupt silence of the motorcycles, and knew something had happened. I went running to see that he was okay and by the time I got there, he was up. But his wheel was bent and damaged and there was no way he could continue the race. My father did file a complaint after the race, but gentleman that he was, he didn't hold a grudge against the reckless competitor who had endangered them both. Instead, he reached out to the man and said, "My friend, all is forgotten." They shook hands and they parted on amiable terms. For me, this was a lesson learned in sportsmanship.

I, too, had a lightweight-class Jawa motorcycle I was given for my birthday that year. I decided to enter a race also, although it wasn't anything like the races my father had done. He had given both Huibert and me lessons in riding years before so we knew something about the machines. I mainly rode it around the neighborhood and decided I could try this race. It was a sort of track with twists and turns and obstacles and such, and somehow I not only made it, but to my surprise more than anyone's, I won my race. I never entered another race; once was enough for me.

Figure 17 **Winning my one and only motorcycle race, in Bandung, in 1951. Photo by Frits van Demmeltraadt, deceased.**

Huibert also raced that day, in a little higher class than my race, and he won, too. In addition to the small trophies and floral wreaths we won, we each received a beautiful crystal cup from the Jawa factory in Czechoslovakia. I still have that cup on display in my office at home.

I learned to drive a car the same way I did the motorcycle, actually, just driving around the neighborhood until I could master it. We had to double-clutch in those days, and that was a little tricky. I used my mother's car, and I watched Jan drive when he took me to school. With those limited experiences plus the few lessons my father gave me, I learned to drive both the motorcycle and the car.

Trouble at home

While we were living in the house in Dennelust, things went sour between my parents. I will never know exactly what happened, but suffice it to say my parents' marriage broke down. I remember an uncomfortable evening when my father announced he would be leaving the house. He went to live with Tante An, a divorced woman who had been friends with them for a long time.

Huibert and I stayed with our mother in the Dennelust house for a time and then moved to live with my mother's brother, Oom Ben, and their sister Tante Marie, and her children, Olga, and Corrie. Jan Bartels moved also, to the home of his future wife, Oije.

I believe my father had asked Jan to keep watch over me because I was invited to Jan and Oije's home often and the three of us played quite a lot of tennis together. I shall always appreciate the loving care this young couple took of me, while they were busy establishing their own life together. Life went on and I saw my father regularly. While my parents didn't get divorced for many years, they never again lived together. My mother eventually moved to Holland along with Tante Marie. My father stayed with An, and when the divorce finally came through a number of years later, they were married.

Sports and athletics

I loved sports at school and especially when we moved to Tante Marie's, I could easily ride my bicycle or motorcycle to school. We had soccer, throwing the javelin, high- and long-jumping, track, and things like that. I loved it all, particularly tennis which I have played my whole life long.

We also had teams for sports which were school-related, including baseball. My friend Walter Burger was captain of our team, I was the catcher, and another friend Boon, was the pitcher. We actually knew nothing about baseball, but we all loved the sport anyway. We had no coach and only a book with rules which we looked at occasionally. We had homemade bats and gloves which were stiff and unbendable, and balls which weren't exactly round. Boon could only throw fast balls, having never learned anything else. When I first began to play I was nervous when I came up to bat. I struggled to concentrate and watch the ball and tried so hard. Finally, I learned how to tone down my nervousness and did manage to hit the ball pretty well. We played for fun mainly and then we joined the Bandung baseball league.

Not having a clue as to who we might be playing on the league, out of the blue there came a team of *Americans*. These were guys who were in the U.S. Air Force and they were in Indonesia to train the Indonesian Air Force in flying and maintenance and general practices. These guys wanted some fun so they joined the local baseball league while they were in our country. Here we were, high school kids who didn't know a thing about really playing baseball, and we were faced with a team of seasoned American pilots who had been playing baseball all their lives.

Not only could they play with strategies and tactics, they had their own equipment with perfect bats, soft leather gloves, and precision balls. We were totally blown away by these "professionals," but we played our hearts out and watched them carefully to learn the game. All we could really do with any accuracy was run like crazy, and we ran as much as we could.

During one game I watched their batter and learned he always hit low. I told Boon to throw the ball at my glove and we'd try to strike him out. That's exactly what he did and the batter missed the ball.

One thing we had learned as youngsters was that the umpire was always right – even if he wasn't. It was a given through the years that we *never* questioned the umpire. This was a form of respect which was deep-rooted in us, and we would never have even considered arguing with the umpire on a perceived wrong call.

After the batter missed the ball from my suggestion to the pitcher, and when the umpire yelled, "Strike!" I silently cheered. Overt cheering, clapping, and yelling was considered bad sportsmanship, and was simply not done. On the other hand, the American girls who had come along with their team immediately started screaming at the umpire. This was shocking to say the least, and we were stunned by their brassy taunts. These ugly, too-casual girls hopping around in their hair curlers and bright red lipstick, were yelling, "Kill the umpire! That wasn't a strike, it was a ball! Kill the umpire!" It not only shocked all of us, it certainly shocked the umpire, too. The umpire, a local Chinese man, was utterly surprised and flustered and didn't know what to do. I turned around just then and I have to say it was the first time I saw a Chinese man with huge, totally round eyes.

Apparently I was known by the Americans to hit the ball to the right field and one time when I came up to bat, I heard their catcher say, "He's a good hitter," and I saw the whole field team shift to the right. I thought to myself I needed to hit to their blank spot. I wasn't quite sure how to do that, so I just turned my body a little bit to the left. The pitcher threw and I turned a little more and hit the ball with all my might straight to left field where there was nobody waiting. This little trick got me all the way to second base. What a joy that was! Of course, we always lost every game we played with the Americans, but we did have a good time – and we most assuredly learned a lot about baseball.

Adventures of a teenage boy

My best friend through high school was Cor Schalks, whose father owned the Lembang Hotel. Cor and I went to high school together at the Lyceum. The Lembang Hotel was an upscale hotel that was more of a resort area with small bungalows, and an attraction for people from the city because they had special events like bands on the weekends. Cor and I took music lessons from a man named de Karls, who was well-known in Bandung because his small band played in the good hotels like the Homan and the Lembang. The teacher played the accordion and I initially played that, too, but eventually I switched to playing the piano. I took lessons from de Karls for more than four years, and I played for my own enjoyment for many years.

Cor, on the other hand, didn't like music lessons and lasted for only a couple of months. He just didn't like to practice. Also, during our lessons de Karls would sit next to us with one hand on the piano by the lowest base notes. He always had a heavy thick pencil between his fingers. He didn't do it to me, but whenever Cor would make a mistake, de Karls would hit Cor's knuckles with his heavy pencil. One day Cor had had enough of the knuckle-banging. He yelled and grabbed the piano cover and slammed it down on the teacher's hand. Needless to say, that was the end of Cor's piano career.

Actually, de Karls was a really good musician. We studied many good composers but most of their works were basically exercises, and these just didn't interest me. De Karls asked me what I really wanted to play, and I said, "The Hungarian Rhapsody." Sure enough, he brought "The Hungarian Rhapsody" piece of music for me to play along with the normal exercises. It was really beautiful and included passages of very intricate notes, and I had a terrible time trying to play it. I tried and tried, but I just couldn't seem to get one passage especially right. De Karls showed me flawlessly how to do it, all the while holding the big pencil in his fingers and never moving from his place at the end of the bench. Eventually I learned to play the piece, but it took a long while.

Sigi was another friend from school. Sigi's mother did cooking for people in the neighborhood and he had the job of delivering the meals. For some reason, some boys started to taunt him and gave him trouble while he was trying to carry the meals on his bike. Huibert and our cousin Humphrey who was living with us then and Cor and I tried to help Sigi from being bullied by the boys, and he was grateful. We became friends, and Sigi liked classical music, so he often came by to listen to me play the piano. Sigi was an Eagle Scout and because of him I also joined and was eventually able to pass all the tests to become an Eagle Scout.

Cor had a little vehicle that belonged to the hotel. It was an early version of the Volkswagen bus. Frequently he would meander by our house at mealtime in his little bus because he loved the Indo *Rijsttafel*, especially cooked by Tante Marie. On the other hand, I really loved the Dutch cuisine with potatoes and all, and the Lembang Hotel featured this type of cooking. As a result, we went to each other's places to eat at least once a week.

Cor had a Jawa motorcycle and I had a smaller Jawa machine. Another friend, Jan Horsting whom I met through Cor, also had a Jawa motorcycle. Along with a couple of others, we had this small group that liked to take motorcycle trips together. We didn't often go away overnight, but especially at vacation time from school, we went on day trips and shorter ones, too.

We always started our day trips from Jan Horsting's house so we could get the weather forecast. Jan's family had an elderly Javanese servant who could predict the weather, and we learned the man was always right on the money with his predictions. It was important for us to know whether it was going to rain if we were going riding because the rains in a tropical climate could be devastatingly heavy. This made riding on dirt roads dangerous. Riding along mountain roads with no guard rails or paving or anything was dangerous enough, but adding torrential rain to a sharp curve on a dirt road could make riding especially treacherous.

The Javanese man at Jan's house seemed to know exactly what

was going to happen. We would all gather there and Jan would ask him if there was going to be rain. The man would walk to the window and look outside briefly. One time when we saw clouds gathering we were sure it would rain, but the man said no, it wouldn't rain that day. We had learned by that time to trust him so off we went and had a great time with no rain. Other times he would say it would rain and he was always specific about the time. For example, he would say, "The day will be fine until two o'clock. Then there will be heavy rain for four hours." He was so accurate with his predictions and knew not only when it would start to rain, but when it would stop. We could plan our trips perfectly around his predictions so we could get home before the rain.

Thinking about this today, with the complex equipment used by meteorologists all over the world to predict the weather, and how often they are wrong, makes this story even more amazing. Here was a simple houseboy who had a natural gift for knowing how to predict the weather. Day after day he told whoever asked what the day would bring, and he was never wrong. It seems sad today to think it would never have occurred to this man to profit from his gift, and I have no doubt he remained a houseboy for the rest of his working life.

The day of the trip as shown in the following photo, the houseboy predicted no rain. We had planned to go up to the volcano, *Tangkuban Perahu*,[10] not far from Bandung, to see the crater. When we drove up the mountain, we saw the gate to the top of the volcano was closed. At about the same time, Cor's motorcycle had a problem and quit running. The motor had overheated by the hard

---

[10] From Wikipedia®: A study conducted in 2001 determined that *Tangkuban Perahu* has erupted at least 30 times in the previous 40,000 years. Most of these were minor eruptions with one as recently as 2013, but nine of them were major. The name *Tangkuban Perahu* translates loosely to "upturned boat" in reference to a local legend about its creation. It is a popular tourist attraction where tourists can hike or ride to the edge of the crater to view the hot water springs and boiling mud up close, and buy eggs cooked on the hot surface.

labor of climbing the mountain road. What happens is the piston expands more than the cylinder does, and it wedges. We had heard you could douse the cylinder with water to cool it off enough to get the engine started again (not smart, but what did we know?). We sat there and blew on the engine a little, but that didn't help. All at once I heard a sizzling noise and saw steam coming from the engine, and there was Cor peeing on the engine. We didn't have water, so he thought he'd try a little natural water. The smell was pretty awful so he didn't do it for long, but ultimately we were lucky. It worked, and the engine started again.

Before turning back, we found out why the gate was closed. *Tangkuban Perahu* is considered a dormant volcano as far as a major eruption, but it does emit gases and steam and boiling mud pretty much all the time. With the huge open crater and steam rising, it's an awesome sight. However, sometimes the poisonous gases get a little overwhelming, and that's what happened. The poison gases were settling in the valleys because of the lack of wind that day, and it was too dangerous to breathe near the crater.[11]

---

[11] A recent example of the dangers of poisonous gases emitted from volcanos is from the trip Gloria and I made to Indonesia in 2005. We were touring a volcanic area in East Java where gases and steam were rising all around us from boiling water and lava. Momentarily appreciating the quiet because the local vendors were not pursuing us here, our group of 70 was innocently scampering around on barely hardened crust near boiling, steam-spitting geysers. We were warned to watch our footing, but looking back on this gravely dangerous activity, we were amazingly lucky to get out without incident. The vendors knew better than to be where we were, and were camped out far from the dangers. We learned later that two weeks before we were there, a group of campers had died overnight from the gases that poisoned them in their sleep.

Figure 18 Our trip to the crater on *Tangkuban Perahu* was cut short because the gate was closed. I am squatting on the left, Jan is on his motorcycle, and Cor is looking at his overheated engine. Note the small *kampong* at the junction in the road. The signs are for eating places in the village, where they sold things like sweet potatoes, fruits, and cookies. Photo by unknown native using my camera.

Another time I went with these same boys and some others to Jakarta. Jan and Cor had friends in Jakarta who had sailing boats. This involved an overnight and the plan was to motorbike to Jakarta, and sail to a small island off the coast and stay there overnight. I can't imagine our parents letting us go off on such a trip, but they must have trusted us. We were all about 15 or 16. The road to Jakarta was considered safer at that time – this was around 1950 – but there was still one spot where rebels had not given up. They had formed their own little gangs of bandits, led by disillusioned Japanese soldiers who had never given up, and now and then they would ambush travelers on the road. For some reason we weren't worried – likely it was the fearlessness of youth – and we happily motored away.

We made it to Jakarta without incident and went to the place to rent sailing boats. We loaded up in two small boats and took off at about three o'clock in the afternoon. A good wind allowed us to sail for about three hours to a small island where there was nothing but sand and jungle. We unloaded and prepared to spend the night. Before we went to sleep we decided to swim a while, and nobody had a swim suit. There we were, eight naked boys frolicking on the beach, splashing in the water and having a great time. However, when it came time to sleep, we realized we had brought nothing but towels. No other sleeping gear, not even any real food. Well, we weren't hungry at that point, so we built a campfire and settled down and started telling stories.

Somebody mentioned we had to be careful because there were scorpions on those islands and they were dangerous. That's all it took to make me certain I wouldn't be doing much sleeping. One of the other guys felt the same way and we sat by the fire talking while the others went a little ways away and slept on the sand. I did try to sleep standing up, but quickly discovered that didn't work. The moment I fell asleep, I started to fall over.

Suddenly, I saw a huge scorpion coming toward me. It was about four inches long not including his tail. I pointed my hunting knife at the scorpion. Quick as lightning, he stung the blade with his tail. We found a can lying there and I stuck the scorpion with my knife and put it in the can. He was still crawling around and when I poked at him I saw even when he was dying he was able to sting. We spent the rest of the night waiting for the scorpion to die, but the moment we touched it, it began to move.

Around midnight, one of the other guys started yelling and everybody else woke up. He said a gigantic rat had walked over his face and woke him up. After that I was determined more than ever not to sleep, and I didn't. I was the only one who didn't sleep at all, because I was too scared. There was no way I could have let down my guard with rats and scorpions and who knows what else lurking in the dark. I kept looking at the scorpion, and toward the morning, I decided to cut him in half and see what happened. After an hour or so I touched the head and his feelers were still searching around. I touched the tail, and bang, the stinger attacked the knife blade.

In the morning, the fire was still going and the scorpion was still moving. Around noon-time we were thinking of leaving, and I decided to upend the can and put the scorpion in the fire, which I did, and I think that was the end of him, although I didn't stay around to find out.

We loaded up the boats and started to sail back to Jakarta. To our dismay, after the brisk wind of the day before, this day there was no wind. Of course, unprepared as we were, there were no paddles in the boats either. There we sat, dead in the water. We managed to find some pots and pans in the boats, so I took the cover of a pan and starting paddling with it. Another guy did the same thing and we managed to make some headway – slowly.

After a while, I was really tired, having no sleep and nothing to eat, but we did have some water along so we had something to drink. I scrunched up and tried to sleep. The sun was burning down on us so I wet my towel in the sea and put it over my head and shoulders. It was so hot that within ten minutes, the towel was bone-dry. In spite of the heat, I dozed off. Sharply, I woke up to the other boys yelling, "Sharks! Sharks!" I jumped up wide awake and we all had our knives ready to defend ourselves. Then we noticed the shark fin wasn't moving. We watched some more, and then paddled over to it and discovered instead of a shark it was a piece of bamboo sticking out of the water.

I was awake now. We kept paddling and came to another small island. On this island was a water buffalo. There was absolutely nothing on the tiny island – no water or anything and we had no idea of how long he had been there. Somebody said the buffalo must be thirsty, because he came right up to us with no fear and looked like he was in great distress. We wanted to help him so we put the rest of our fresh water in a pan and held it out to him. He drank it in a moment and was looking for more.

Shortly after finding the water buffalo, we saw a motorboat with some Indonesians in it. The people saw all the commotion with our two small sailboats there and the buffalo. We all knew the animal was too big to fit into any of our boats, but it needed to get off the island to survive. In the end, the people in the motorboat tied a rope around the buffalo's horns and pretty much dragged it through the sea to Jakarta, and we never saw it again. Later we heard some Indonesians were transporting some animals, and the buffalo must have fallen off their barge and swam to the island and became stranded. We never knew if the people in the motorboat were the owners of the animal or if they just happened to come by.

Meanwhile, we were still paddling away through the windless day. After starting out from the island shortly after noon, we finally got to Jakarta after five o'clock. The wind started picking up about four, so we did get a little help with sailing, but it was a long day. After landing, we returned our sailboats and headed for the roadside vendors for something to eat. This was something we were continuously told not to do by all of our families because of not knowing what we were eating or how it was prepared, but we were starved at that point. Actually, I ate at the roadside vendors all the time as a kid and I never got sick in spite of my parents' warnings. I guess forbidden food tastes better and we sure enjoyed it. After we stuffed ourselves, we got on our motorbikes and headed home, fortunately, without further incidents.

Chapter 7

The Spirit World

Indonesia's mystical culture

Many Hindu-Buddhist mythical beings have a role in Javanese and Balinese mythology. When Islam came to the Indonesian archipelago, additional devils, angels, and demons were added to the mix. Belief in local spirits such as the forest guardian, the ghost of water or haunted places still exists, often associated with a jinn, an Islamic spiritual creature, or the tormented soul of a deceased human.

Life in the United States, a younger society that is based on Christian beliefs of love and kindness, is a completely different experience than everyday life in the environment where I grew up. Even though we were a Christian family with Christian friends and acquaintances, the overpowering culture was mystical. Living in a country with ancient roots and thousands of years of supernatural and sorcerous practices taught me first-hand that you don't mess with Indonesia's mystical culture. This shadowy culture is physically and spiritually evident, daily, and there is no denying its presence. Some of my own experiences are told here and they are but an insignificant few of the many paranormal events that take place continually in daily life in Indonesia.

Bird of death

The *piet-van-vliet* (pronounced pete-von-fleet) is a common bird found in Indonesia, the Philippines, southern China and other nearby areas. It is a small wailing cuckoo. The name, *piet-van-vliet*, is the sound of the bird's call. The bird is a brood parasite, which means the female lays her eggs in the nests of various other small birds instead of building her own. The belief in Indonesia is when the *piet-van-vliet* sings from a tree in your yard, that someone will die very soon in that house. This causes anyone who hears the cuckoo's call to look carefully to see from where the sound is coming.

I heard the bird calling many times in my youth, and always cautiously looked to see where it was perched. Ominously, only once was it wailing from a tree in our yard. Sad but true, it was the day my beloved nanny Maktje unexpectedly died.

Wayang

Wayang is the generic term for Indonesian puppetry theater. *Wayang* comes from the Indonesian word for shadow, *bayang.* The shadow puppets are figures made from water buffalo hide or wood, and *wayang* could be the world's oldest puppet form, dating back to the 800s. Becoming a puppeteer takes seven to eight years of study and is an extremely honorable position, equal to the most highly educated professionals. This person usually carves their own puppets in the beginning, and performs from memory all of the parts in a performance, while operating the puppets.

When Gloria and I were in Indonesia in 2005, we visited a *kampong* and met a puppeteer who told of his extensive education and training to become a recognized puppeteer. He sat in his grass-roofed hut amid dozens of finished and partially finished hand-crafted wooden puppets, and spoke with great pride of his profession. His own wizened face was surrounded by the puppets' frozen expressions of sadness, gladness, terror and joy.

From him, we learned the clown or jester is an important part of the cast of characters in all *wayang* plays. In Indonesia, the clown is the only individual who can speak aloud of political events. Apparently, people are not allowed to talk among themselves in the villages about politics, and the only way they can find out about what's going on is to listen to the puppets. Many villages have *wayang* performances which last late into the night for several nights in a row. This brings entertainment galore to the villagers, plus a little covert information about their country's political situation they are eager to hear. Of course, this is an additional burden on the puppeteer. Not only must he know the ancient stories thoroughly, he must always be current on political movements as well. He has to know how to deliver the news, good and bad, in the most discreet and diplomatic way possible.

Figure 19 Wayang puppets of the Wayang golek, or wooden type. Puppeteers hold the puppet by a central wooden rod, and use wooden handles to move the puppets' hands for the performance. Photo by Gloria VanDemmeltraadt

There are several forms of puppetry: *wayang kulit*, which uses shadow puppets with the puppets performing behind a back-lighted sheet; *wayang golek*, three-dimensional wooden puppets, primarily used in West Java; and *wayang orang*, which are not puppets, but real people playing the roles of wayang.

One of the plays performed by the *wayang* is called the *Ramayana*, and it depicts a royal family and its many adventures. We saw a play performed by real actors in the *wayang orang* format during our trip in 2005. The story told about a princess who was stolen by bad monkeys and whisked away to the forest. It is up to the prince to rescue her, amid many perils. Most of the *wayang* plays follow a similar theme, with an evil entity that threatens the royals in a variety of ways, but good always triumphs in the end.

In many villages, the *wayang* plays might be accompanied by the often eerie sounds of a *gamelan* orchestra. *Gamelan* is the overall term for an orchestra composed of instruments including metallic "drums" of various sizes which are struck with a mallet. *Gamel* is a low Indonesian word for mallet. Other instruments in the orchestra can include the metallophone, or xylophone, tuned metal bars struck with a mallet, and bamboo flutes.

In Javanese mythology, the *gamelan* was created in AD 230 by the god who ruled as king of all Java. He needed a signal to summon the gods and thus invented the gong. For more complex messages, he invented two other gongs, thus forming the original *gamelan* set.[12]

Voodoo

Voodoo, with what they call black magic and the white magic that counteracts certain activities, has been practiced in Indonesia for centuries. As an example, one of my cousins suddenly took sick, and developed a fever and quickly got sicker and sicker over several days.

---

[12] R.T. Warsodiningrat, *Serat Weda Pradangga*. Cited in Roth, A. R. *New Compositions for Javanese Gamelan.* University of Durham, Doctoral Thesis, 1986. Page 4, via Wikipedia®

A regular doctor was called in and could find nothing wrong. The family called a witch doctor, called a *dukun*, who discovered under my cousin's mattress, a bunch of herbs and spices wrapped in a banana leaf and speared with bamboo pins. He removed the poisonous ball, her bedding was cleaned, and she immediately recovered. They never found out who put the malicious concoction there, but this was certainly evidence of the practice of black magic. The malevolent practice doesn't always follow a purely spiritual avenue, but as in this case, makes use of compositions of natural elements.

Another event that did go along a spiritual path involved my mother and her brother Ben who were once with a group of young people on holiday from school or work and they were all staying at my grandparents' home. The group went for a walk in the afternoon through the *sawas* (rice fields). As they were about to enter a forest, an old man suddenly appeared in the middle of their path. He told them not to go into the forest because it was sacred ground and inhabited by spirits. With this tantalizing warning, the young people couldn't possibly keep from going into the forest. They bypassed the man and sauntered through the forest enjoying the breeze through the trees and nothing strange seemed to happen.

At the other end of the forest they looked up a steep hill and saw a road with some traffic. When they saw a car coming by, one of them suggested it would be fun to pretend to cry for help and see what the people would do.

They loudly yelled "Help!" three times and the car stopped. People got out of the car to see what was going on. The young folks hid and laughed when the people searched and called out. Finally, after much calling and searching for someone in distress, the people went back to their car and drove on.

The teens went back to my grandparents' house, ate dinner and went to bed. During the night one of the girls from the group became ill with a high fever. The others woke up and tried to keep her in bed but she insisted she needed to get up and go outside. She said there was a handsome man outside who was calling her to join him. By this time everyone in the house was awake and they tried to call a doctor for the girl, but the phone wouldn't work. They then decided to take her to the doctor, but their car wouldn't start, nor would any other cars at the house.

The girl was Roman Catholic so they decided to pray. Ben was a spiritually strong person and wanted to pray with the girl's own rosary. They looked in her purse where she always kept her rosary, but no one could find it. All the while, the girl was fighting to get outside to reach the handsome man who she believed wanted to talk to her. No one else saw or heard anything outside.

Not having the rosary, Ben decided to read to her from the Bible to try to calm her down. The girl wouldn't let him read and kept saying that the man outside had a better book and wanted her to join him. Ben instead started to pray the Lord's Prayer with the girl, and as soon as he began, she got very agitated. She was now struggling to get out of the bed, but the others were holding her down.

Meanwhile, during the melee, the grandmother in the house had sent a servant to the *kampong* for a voodoo doctor, or *dukun* to come. The *dukun* came and sat next to the bed on the floor while the girl was struggling. He burned some incense to help him connect with the spiritual world and seemed to go into a trance as he listened. The *dukun* asked the group if they had gone into the forest and called for help three times as a prank. The young people admitted they had. The *dukun* then said the spirit told him, "No help is forthcoming," and the man got up and left the house.

Ben kept trying to get the girl to pray with him, but she didn't want to do it. He fought with her and struggled for several minutes more. Finally, in a belligerent voice, she said quickly, "Our Father!" She then made horrible faces and grimaces. After more struggles he tried to get her to repeat "Who art in heaven," and after a long while, she growled, "Who art in heaven," with more grimaces.

Suddenly she looked up at Ben and yelled, "Ben, watch out!" The girl ducked and said, "He dives at you with a spear!" Ben sank to his knees and kept praying in a loud voice, and the girl cried out about an "air battle" taking place between an angel who had come to intercept the attack by a demon. She ducked and bobbed around for several minutes, and her agitation was powerfully intense.

Finally, still in a fast and belligerent voice, she yelled "Hallowed be thy name!" Instantly, the tension flowed out of the room and the girl calmed down completely. A peaceful expression came over her face as she stretched out on the bed and calmly finished saying the prayer to the end, and promptly fell asleep. When all was quiet, the rest of the group went to bed also.

The next morning everyone was well. In addition, the telephone worked, the cars all started, and the lost rosary was found in the girl's purse. Were these three suspicious events in return for three false calls for help? No one will ever know.

Superstition follows both fact and fantasy in most cultures. Indonesia abounds with mystical happenings and whether fantasy or fact, my own experiences have taught me great respect for the paranormal. I describe below several other mystical events that helped to reinforce that respect.

Strange things

Strange things began to happen soon after we moved to the house in Dennelust, a fairly new housing area in Bandung, after we returned from Holland in 1948. It's difficult for me to talk about even today, because others might not understand how strange and just plain creepy some of these events were.

My first recognition of something odd was to see dark shadowy flashes in my peripheral vision (in Dutch I would say "in the corner of my eyes"). I would be walking in the house, or sitting quietly doing my homework, and suddenly a black shadow would flit by. Along with this was a dark and heavy feeling. I'd quickly turn my head and nothing would be there. At first I thought this might be something in my eye, an eyelash or piece of dust or something, but it wasn't. I was really seeing something for a fleeting moment, something black and sinister flashing by.

Then I started to hear music. At night, in bed, I would unexpectedly begin to hear complete symphonies reverberating in my head. We had no radio and there was no way I could be hearing music coming from another source. The neighbors were too far away. This experience was quite pleasant, if odd. I loved music and when I got over my surprise at hearing it, the beautiful music would often lull me to sleep. I was the only one who heard these beautiful concerts, and often thought if I was a composer I could become famous by writing down the melodies. This experience lasted off and on for the whole time we lived in that house.

One of the "perks" of having our father own an automobile and motorcycle dealership was that both Huibert and I had our own motorcycles. From the age of 15, I used my motorcycle daily to get to school and sports and everywhere I needed to go. The road to our house was not straight. It went up and down with many curves, and went down into a valley with a *sawa* all around. One day on my way home, I was in the valley and I clearly heard my name being called in a shrill woman's voice. I stopped at the bottom of the valley and looked around but saw no one. When I got home I told my mother about hearing the woman. She looked very serious and told me sternly if ever I heard my name being called in that way again, to not answer, quickly get out of there, and not look back.

My room on the second floor of our house had a window to the back of the house where there was a stone staircase. The steps led up to a covered walkway and a balcony and a door to the house. Beneath the balcony was a storeroom. The second floor bathroom where I showered was near the doorway. I remember several incidents when after I showered and went back to my room, I had a strong feeling of being watched. There was never anything or anyone on the walkway outside, but I couldn't shake the feeling someone was watching me. One day a maid found a snake in my bathroom, which was odd. Snakes don't like cold and it would be abnormal for one to climb the cold stone steps outside. We never found out how the snake got in there, but it was removed and after that I didn't have the feelings of being watched.

One evening I went into my room and turned on the light, and suddenly a hazy illuminated ball floated in the middle of the room. The ball immediately exploded with a crisp puff, and a curl of white smoke spread over the room. I screamed and within three jumps I was downstairs where my mother was. She could see something had happened and when I told her about the smoke, she said, "It's too bad you didn't catch it!"

As I learned later, smoke is a common occurrence with spirits. It is said that if you instantly catch the smoke in a jar and clap on the lid, you have captured the evil spirit and it can no longer hurt you. Fortunately, this never happened to me again, as I can't say I'm in the habit of carrying a jar everywhere I go.

Premonitions

When I was about 14 years old, I began to have unsettling premonitions. Entire scenes would play in my head with people moving and talking and things happening, and I knew with complete certainty these scenes were really going to happen. One example is going with my father to Jakarta to the General Motors assembly plant. Waiting for him there, Huibert and I were outside looking around. In a village square with grass and trees, a car started to back up into the street on the other side of the grassy square. Out of nowhere I knew exactly what was going to happen. I could see in my mind that a truck would come around the corner and there would be a traffic jam. I knew the drivers would hang out of their windows and talk to each other and I knew the car would go first and the truck would then go back into the street and its brakes would squeak loudly. It was a simple and innocent scene. No one got hurt or anything and there was no damage, but I could see the whole thing happening in my mind in color, all before it happened.

After this scene I had other similar premonitions and they got more menacing each time. One strange forewarning was sometime in 1949.

Our two-story house was quite spacious, with many rooms. Huibert slept on the main floor and all of our dogs also slept in his room. We had five dogs at the time, two belonged to Jan Bartels, and three were ours. All were friendly, happy dogs. Our house lot was about three-quarters of an acre, with a four-foot-high chain link fence around our back yard, useful for keeping all of the dogs at home.

One normal evening, on the way to my upstairs bedroom, I placed my foot on the first step, and abruptly, I froze. I was completely stopped from going any farther, and I absolutely could not move my foot to the next step. I suddenly had what can only be called an insight – a message from somewhere that something terrible was going to happen – not at that time, but I knew it would be in the middle of the night. I heard in my mind exactly what was going to happen, and knew I would be awakened by a terrible rattling. I can hear the sound now in my mind, as I heard it with my foot on the first step so long ago. It was a choking sound from something or someone in a desperate death battle. The feeling was strong enough to stop my path up the stairs, but apparently not strong enough for me to tell anyone else about it. I finally overcame the blockage of my steps, and thinking I was imagining things, went on up to bed.

At two o'clock in the morning I was awakened by exactly the sound I had heard in my mind earlier in the evening. It was a horrible, loud, strangled sound made by something non-human which seemed to be choking. The sound came from outside, and I leaped out of bed. With quivering legs I went to the window, grabbing a machete on the way. I was ready for action!

The terrible sound woke everyone else in our house, and the neighbors, too. People were soon milling about looking for the source of the screaming. It turned out the neighbors' dog had tried to jump the fence into our yard. He was on a leash and the chain was too short to reach over the fence, causing the dog to hang in mid-air. His strangled screams split the night as if it had been cut by my machete.

Before long, the neighbors rescued their dog, which did live through the adventure, although he must have had a very sore throat for a few days, and everyone went back to bed.

These situations began to frighten me and I finally had enough of this. I didn't like the feelings I had when these premonitions came over me and the feelings got more and more unsettling. The events foretold became increasingly disturbing and predicted bad things to happen. One day I threw up my hands and yelled out loud, "That's enough – I'm through with you – be gone!" And that was the end of them. It was like something passed out of me – away from me – and I never had another premonition again.

Dogs in the corner

Another event that involved our dogs wasn't really a premonition, but a strange event nonetheless. Our five dogs at the time included a mother with four of her offspring, older than pups. They were a sort of cocker spaniel mix, certainly not the brightest of beasts, but protective of us, and much treasured by all. One dark evening the dogs were lying on the floor between the open door to the terrace and the dining table where my mother and I were sitting while she helped with my school work. All were "people" dogs who loved to drape themselves wherever we happened to be.

Suddenly the entire gang of five bounded up at the same time as if awakened from a terrifying nightmare. Neck hair up, legs and ears stiff, grunting and trembling, almost screaming in their growls, they formed a semi-circle and approached the corner of the room near the rear door. They approached as one and suddenly backed up, obviously very afraid of something in the corner. My shouts to calm them were not heard. I suspected a scorpion or snake or something, and I first looked on the terrace and there was nothing there, nor was there anything to see in the corner. The dogs kept up their crying and now feeling a little anxious, I crept closer. I saw or smelled nothing but suddenly seemed to have the same frightening feeling as the dogs. The hair on my arms rose and the closer I got to the corner, the more

I sensed the presence of something dark and fearsome. I heard my mother utter a sound – perhaps a prayer, something she was good at doing – and the entire scene lasted only a few moments. Almost as abruptly as it began, it stopped. Like snow melting in the sun, the anxious feelings disappeared. The dogs calmed and laid down to continue their snoozing and everything went back to normal. As can be guessed, no cause was ever found for the strange feelings.

The faith healer

During the time we lived in the Dennelust house, my parents were having marital difficulties. Also, my mother was having continual problems with asthma. I have never in my life seen anyone have such severe attacks of asthma, and she had many hospital stays for breathing problems.

No doubt my mother tried everything she possibly could to get relief from her asthma. A local man was recommended to her by some friends, and I expect she was desperate to try anything. The man was an Indo and he was a sort of doctor, but more of a faith healer. My understanding is he did not touch her in his treatments. Instead, he held his hands high over her and moved from her head to her feet and then shook his hands out. Later she said she could feel something like prickling needles throughout her body as his hands moved. At first she had some good results from these treatments and she continued to go to the man's house and sometimes he came to our home.

One thing he did was to determine whether there were "harmful earth rays" in our house. He came to the house to make sure all of our beds and furniture were correctly oriented. If they were not as he specified, he moved the furniture himself, especially the beds, to align them with the proper "earth rays." He even made suggestions for our dogs – this was when our mother dog was expecting her litter of four – and when the time came, he cut the puppies' tails and cropped their ears according to their mixed cocker spaniel breed. He was a pretty handy guy all around, I guess.

One day I was asked to deliver something to this man's house. While I was there he asked me if I wanted to see a picture of the devil. Being a young teenager, of course I was curious and wanted to see it. He showed me a black and white photograph of an indoor room with furniture and a vague background. Then he showed me another picture with the same background, but swirling in the middle of the picture was a curl of white smoke. It didn't look like much to me, and I thought this was nonsense but he said it was the devil.

Oddly, not long after I saw the picture, was the event in my bedroom when I turned on the light and there was the floating fuzzy ball in the middle of the room. That occurrence by itself would have been frightening, but having seen the picture previously, it was terrifying.

One day my mother was leaving the healer's place after a treatment. Before she left, he said to her, "Mrs. van Demmeltraadt, you have to be careful today." When she asked why, he said, "You might get in an accident on the way home, but don't worry, I will protect you."

My mother usually drove herself around town and she was a very careful and slow driver, but with this advice, she drove even slower on the way home. There was a long lazy curve in the road along the way, nothing sharp or dangerous, but somehow her car, a medium-sized German car called an Adler, flipped over in the curve.

Curiously, the car didn't flip as one would expect it to do on the outside of the curve, but it tipped over on the inside of the curve which makes no sense at all. But tip it did, and it was quite a crash. Some military men who were nearby heard it happen and ran to help, thinking the driver must be hurt. Instead, up popped my mother out of the open window as the car lay on its side, and she greeted them with a cheery "Hello!" She was completely unhurt and these big Dutch soldiers were dumbfounded, expecting to find the driver crumpled inside the car, or possibly even dead.

Later, she told me she was driving carefully along the road and suddenly she saw a flash of light in front of her and heard a loud bang, and the windshield of the car exploded. The next thing she knew the car was tipped over. The military men saw and heard nothing unusual until they heard the crash.

This event led all of us, especially my mother, to trust the healer even more. He had obviously protected her from being hurt in this accident. Looking back now, I am stunned at the level of trust we had in this man, who was strange to say the least.

It was during his treatment of my mother over a couple of years, when many of the abnormal events I have talked about occurred. I have my suspicions as to who or what caused them, but we will never know for sure. Several things happened in a relatively short time to confuse everything, one being that my father left the house. About the end of 1950, he moved out to be with the woman with whom he had been having a relationship. About the same time, the rest of us moved away from the Dennelust house and we lived with my Tante Marie and her children.

The last event a few months later was the death of the faith healer. We never found out how or why, but a member of his family came to our house to say he had suddenly died.

Strangely, the night the man died, I had gone to church with my Oom Ben. My family is Christian, but Oom Ben was the one who seemed to be the most faithful because he went to church often while the rest of us did not. Anyway, this night he had invited me to go with him and I did. Sitting in the pew, I happened to be looking at the large blank wall behind the minister, and I suddenly began to get very anxious. I was worried about the healer, specifically, that he might die and leave us unprotected. What would happen to us if we didn't have his protection? When we went home we were met at the door by my mother who told us someone had died. I knew immediately who it was and was not surprised when she revealed the name.

During the time we knew this man, he had professed to doubt his belief in God. He most definitely had some supernatural abilities, difficult as they might be to explain. However, my mother told me she had heard when he died his last words were, "God forgive me."

Being a Christian man, I can only be thankful he called on God at the last moment, and I wish him well in the hereafter.

After we moved away from the Dennelust house and the faith healer died, the supernatural events which seemed to be plaguing our family abruptly stopped.

Chapter 8

The End and the Beginning

My career objectives

In Holland in 1947, before we went back to Indonesia, my father came one evening to speak about what I wanted to do with my life. Not having given it a lot of thought, I said I might like to be a minister or maybe a lawyer. Carefully thinking, he didn't want to say these were bad choices, but he did eventually say when difficult times come – alluding to the Japanese occupation – these types of jobs are the first to be eliminated. They aren't needed for basic survival. The way he said it was, "Those are the first to die." He said the jobs that stay are those which are useful; the ones which have a purposeful function.

His advice echoed in my head and when I got into high school I decided being an engineer would be a purposeful function. I began to focus on engineering as a potential career.

Off to Holland again

In 1953, I finished high school with the qualifications I needed to attend college. We had no graduation ceremonies then; classes just ended like they did after each school year. About a month before my 18th birthday, I flew to Holland alone, to start my college training. Little did I know then, I would never again live in Indonesia.

Tante Fie and Oom Anton picked me up at the Schiphol airport and I spent the summer with them before I started college in September. They drove me to Dordrecht in southern Holland and helped me get registered and ready for college.

The year before I left for college in Holland, Huibert had gone to Munich, Germany to work for a year in the BMW factory. The plan for him at that time was that after gaining experience in the automotive field he would go back to Indonesia and work with our father.

A month or so after I arrived in Holland, Jan Bartels and his wife Oije came to Holland, and the three of us decided to visit Huibert in Munich. We always had quite a good time together and thought we'd have some fun. All four of us for whatever reason decided we'd go to a strip club for the evening. This was my first time in such a place, and I don't know why, but the sights at this club were a lot different than the common sights of topless native girls were while we were growing up. It was pretty exciting. Anyway, we were all dancing and having a good time. Sometime during the evening I was dancing with Oije and there were a bunch of wrestlers in the club who were also dancing. These were huge muscled guys and I happened to bump into one of them. All he did was flex his muscles, and I went flying, clutching Oije in my arms. Somehow we managed to stay upright, and there was a lot of laughter. Just to be sure the muscle-men didn't get upset, we left promptly, but we sure had a good time.

College in Dordrecht

The college I attended was called MTS (Middle Technical School) Dordrecht. About a year later, the school's name was changed to HTS (Higher Technical School). In Holland, universities were for obtaining master's degrees, and schools like the one I attended were to get a bachelor's degree, which was my goal.

This school concentrated on engineering and they had a relationship with companies in Indonesia to train engineers to

operate sugar plantations. Many students at the school were from
Indonesia and some of them were Indos, like me, so that's how we
decided I would go there.

I got a list of room and boarding houses from the college and
I settled in one where there were older students, a year or so ahead
of me. There were three of us per room, and I became friends with
one of my roommates, a tall, blond, blue-eyed Dutch boy, Ewoud
Zuring from Noordwijk. We were only there for a few months and
moved to another boarding house. This house was owned by a young
couple with a child and two rooms to let. We took one, and a man
who eventually became a life-long friend, John Meeder, took the
other room.

My first year at college was not good – at least academically. I
guess the first problem was I never opened a book. There I was in a
new place all by myself and meeting new guys and making friends.
I was just having too much fun to think about studying. At the
beginning of the year, everyone in the school had to assemble in
front of the main building. Then the people were called out by class –
fourth-year, third-year, and so on. When the only ones left were the
first-year students, I looked around and there was my childhood
friend Bonthy Kiliaan. We were delighted to meet up again. Bonthy
had taken a longer course at our high school in Bandung, and I
finished up ahead of him, but now we were entering college at the
same time.

Kattebak

I decided it would be fun to join the fraternity at college, and so
did my Dutch roommate, Ewoud, and Bonthy, too. The fraternity
seemed like a good way to meet friends and besides, the brothers
wore these really great red berets with a yellow puff on top to make
them stand out.

At our school you pledged to join the fraternity and basically after
a one-month hazing period, you were in. The hazing itself was quite

different from what I understand it is in the U.S. and other places. The older guys were not allowed to touch or hurt the new guys, or hit them or anything like that. However, there was a lot of what I call debating and verbal abuse. The process was designed to mentally break us down. We had to sit on the floor in front of the older guys and they would shout and cuss us out, and we were called "pigs," forced to grovel in front of the older guys, and submit to even more verbal abuse.

One example is that an older man would put his feet on my shoulders while I was sitting on the floor in front of him. He would then tell me to make a convincing case for him to remove his feet from my shoulders. I wasn't allowed to say it was inhumane because he would insist I was far, far from human. Justice and equality were also not acceptable reasons because I wasn't worth it. And the debate would go on with him demeaning me and me trying to defend myself.

Most of this occurred in the mess hall area and it went on from maybe seven in the evening until ten or so and then some of the older boys would take the younger ones home. One time there was a "parade of the pigs," and we had to dress in costume. I remember one guy who was dressed as Charlie Chaplin and he looked really great. I was dressed as the Zandvoort Virgin, in a big dress and obviously pregnant. We had to march, and we also had to pull a carriage which carried the committee in charge of handling the whole hazing process, about four or five older boys. During the march the other fraternity brothers would walk along side and in addition to the insults, they threw rotten fruit and other things at us, so at least we learned to dodge.

There were several Indo professors at the school. One of them had a boarding house where Bonthy and a couple of other Indo guys boarded. Rob Ingenluyff and Dick Schrijvers van Zenden were older fraternity brothers there and one evening during the hazing period they approached a bunch of us new guys – pigs at that time – and one of them asked me, "Do you like rice, pig?" Well, I suspected a trap, but I said, "Sure I do!" He then invited me to sit at the table where there was a really good rice dish. I felt guilty eating it because the other pigs were still sitting on the floor, but I ate it. He might have done something to the dish before I ate it, but I'll never know. It tasted good to me.

On the last evening there was a cabaret and the new members had to perform on stage some sort of act for the older guys. We had to tell jokes or play a musical instrument or something, and doing anything was difficult because there was a lot of shouting and cat calls and derogatory remarks. I don't even remember what I did for my performance – most likely played the piano – but I did get through it all and that was the main goal.

After we made it through the hazing process, there was a ball with ladies and dancing, and we new members graduated from being pigs to being full fraternity brothers and well on our way to becoming "old men" like our seniors. In all, it was a good time and I met many really nice people through the whole process – in addition to learning how to drink beer – a lot of beer.

Figure 20 I sent this picture to my father from college thinking he would see all was well. I learned later he agonized over the liquor bottles and the beer I'm holding. It likely prompted the eventual humbling visit with the banker. I proudly took the picture myself using a timer.

After we became full members of the fraternity, Dick and Rob were talking with Bonthy about there being quite a few Indo boys who had nowhere to go during holidays and such, not being able to go home all the way to Indonesia. They decided to form a small group from the fraternity for mostly Indo boys. They talked about the old Navy days where the guys from a ship were divided into smaller groups that were called a "*bak*," which meant "box." Then each "*bak*" got its own name. Apparently there was a much-loved cat at the boarding house where Dick, Rob, and Bonthy lived, so they decided to call our special Indo group the "Kattebak," after "*katte*" which means "cat." After we fashioned the Kattebak, other smaller groups of "*baks*" formed for other groups of young men within the fraternity.

The members of the Kattebak started with Dick, Rob, and Bonthy. The rest of us were specially invited; I made four, and John Meeder and Boyd van den Kieboom joined us, plus René van Aalst, Piet van der Goes, Max van Leeuwen, and Hans van de Water, Gerard Schwencke, and several other guys. After I was gone from school, some others joined the group through the years, some Indo and some Dutch. Ultimately, there were about 18 to 20 men who were part of the Kattebak. These men, along with their wives, have faithfully held reunions through the years, coming from all points of the world. In June of 2014 Gloria and I were there in Holland to celebrate our joyous 60th reunion along with nine original Kattebakers and seven guests. Our school has been torn down now, but we had a wonderful time catching up on our lives and sharing memories.

Vacation in France

In addition to the Kattebak brothers who have remained my true friends through all these years, I made other friends at school, and one was Harry Looman, a fraternity brother, and a member of my mechanical engineering class.

At the end of my first year of school, I received my grades as did everyone else. As I said before, I neglected to ever open a book and my grades were correspondingly bad in most of my classes. The overall result was I flunked my first year of college. The rule was at our school, if you flunked any portion of the year, you had to take the whole year over again. It was like it didn't count at all. Harry had passed his classes and eventually went on to his second year of mechanical engineering. I took a different path.

It happened that Harry had a motorcycle, and now it was vacation time with school finished for the year, so he said, "Hey, would you like to go to southern France with me for the summer?" Well, this sounded like a great idea to me. School was out, nothing else to do, so why not?

Meanwhile, after hearing about my grades, I got notice that my father wanted to meet with me at the end of the summer in Amsterdam at the office of a business friend of his. However, the end of summer was a long way off and there was plenty of time to have some fun, so Harry and I made plans for a great trip.

Engineers both, we constructed a magnificent luggage rack attached to the rear wheel axel on the back of Harry's pre-WWII Belgian motorcycle, an FN. We had our tent, luggage and all supplies loaded on the rack and strapped down and the whole thing was fantastically engineered.

Then came the day when we eager world travelers were ready to depart from Harry's home. His family and neighbors lined up to see us off.

We were proudly dressed for travel including our red fraternity berets. We jumped on the motorcycle and Harry gave a little too much gas as we were waving goodbye. Suddenly the front wheel rose up from all the weight on the back and we careened around the corner and barely hung on till we came to a stop. Out of sight of the family, we unloaded and reloaded everything we had and somehow managed to get it all back together so both wheels stayed on the ground, and off we went.

It took us about a week to get to Nice, and then to Cannes. We camped in our tent and the weather was beautiful on the French Rivera. For about a month, we frolicked in the Mediterranean and drank beer and French wine, and generally had a wonderful time. I must add also, the girls were gorgeous.

Summer was ending and we started thinking of getting ready to go home. That's when the rack on the motorcycle broke and we needed to find a welder. No one is in a hurry in France. When we finally did find a welder, he saw us coming, shut his door and said he was closing for lunch. A couple of hours later he came back and looked at the rack, exclaiming that he needed extra tools and pieces of metal to fix it and we'd have to come back tomorrow.

By this time I realized there was no way I could be back in Amsterdam in time to meet with my father for our session with his banker. Harry and I decided as long as we were going to be delayed anyway, we might as well check out the casino which happened to be nearby in Monaco. While there, I sent a telegram to my father to explain that I couldn't make our meeting. I can only imagine his thoughts on getting a telegram from a casino in Monaco from his indigent son who had just flunked his first year of college and now was unable to make a business meeting with his father and wanted a week's extension.

The meeting

I wasn't worried about the meeting in any way. I was eager to see my father, of course, and when we finally did connect in Amsterdam, I was excited to tell him about my year, and happily entered the somber-looking office building. The mood darkened as soon as I saw the meeting room. It was an exceedingly formal business office with dark oppressive mahogany paneling and books from floor to ceiling. The banker sat behind his enormous desk with a deep frown on his face, and my father's expression was equally serious as they motioned me to sit before them for what was obviously to be – the interrogation.

The first question was about how things were going in Dordrecht. "Well, not so good," I said. We talked about my poor grades and when they asked why I didn't seek tutoring, I said I didn't know about it. Then my father said, "How much money do you have left?"

I took out my billfold and counted five or six guilders, which was basically nothing. He then asked, "Well, how about your savings account?"

"Savings account?"

"Yes, your savings account. Each month I have sent more than a generous amount to cover your expenses and have expected you would put the excess in a savings account."

"Well, I didn't seem to have any left over at the end of each month, what with fraternity expenses and all, so I don't have any savings account," I answered with wavering confidence.

My father's eyebrows rose further and further. With never a harsh word, but using logic only, as was his way, he brought me to understand my foolhardiness. At the end of it, I stood naked before the man and felt lower than a snake's belly, as they say. I meekly agreed to Pa's suggestion of setting up a new account. When school started, I was to get my expense money directly from the banker in Dordrecht, and any extra I might need had to be negotiated with said taciturn banker – the bank president no less – who would maintain close contact with my father. In addition, I was to immediately contact the school for tutoring in my chosen field of mechanical engineering, and my grades would be monitored. And by the way, a new boarding house would be found that didn't put me in such close contact with my fraternity brothers.

College, year two

Properly chastised, I returned to school in the fall, and applied myself diligently to my studies. The amazing thing I discovered was when I actually read the books and listened to lectures, it all made sense. On top of it all, I also learned how to manage money and gained the amazing satisfaction of having money in the bank, a glorious feeling I've appreciated my whole life!

My new boarding house was with the van Slooten family, friends of my father. The van Slootens also had four kids and they ultimately became life-long friends, especially Bas and Renske. I stayed at their house for two years, and through that time I made friends with the Vriesman family, and their daughter Marjanne, the beautiful Dutch girl I eventually married.

A war story

Dordrecht is one of the oldest cities in Holland. The city itself is basically an island, so there are many canals crisscrossing the city. Many of the older houses within the city walls have access to a cobblestone street in the front, and in the back is a canal. These houses have a little pier or dock in the back, with steps going from a door in the lowest floor down to a platform at the water. Of course, the water level rises and falls with the tides.

The Vriesman house was at least three stories high and very large, and was situated on a prominent cobblestone street and a canal. Marjanne's father's name was Jan, which stood for Johannes, and his family was friendly with the van Slooten family where I eventually boarded. Of course, I didn't know firsthand what happened in Holland under the Germans during the war because I was in Indonesia under the Japanese. This story is pieced together from Marjanne's memories and what she was told of the events. The beauty of this story is there are hundreds more like it in the memories of others who survived the war. It speaks of compassion and kindness, qualities which help us all survive.

Marjanne was about four years old when WWII broke out. Her family, including her sisters, Trudy and Lisbeth, plus her father and stepmother, and step sister Anja, lived in the big house. Marjanne's father owned a canning factory in the nearby small town of Zwijndrecht across the river, and they preserved things like pickles, jams, and syrups. When the war broke out, unknown to his family, Jan Vriesman became a member of what they called the "underground," or "the resistance." It became apparent the Jews were being persecuted, and people who were part of the resistance helped the Jews as they could. Having the factory, Jan Vriesman could find room there to hide people as needed. As time went on he hid many Jewish people until they were helped to get away and out of the country. Things went well for a while until one of the Jews sheltered there decided, perhaps for his own gain, to betray the whole operation. It isn't known how he did this, but somehow all of the Jews who were staying there were arrested and most likely never seen again, including the betrayer.

After this, the factory was not a safe place, and the lives of Vriesman and some others were in peril also, having been affiliated with the building and the operation. They had to go underground along with the Jews because they were now being sought. They managed to elude capture for some time. However, one day Jan went to his house to get more supplies or something, and it happened to be the day when their neighborhood was picked for a German *razzia*, which is where the German patrol comes with a lot of manpower and trucks and they search the houses. They would pick up people at random and arrest them, creating fear and panic.

They came to the Vriesman house, and Jan had to quickly hide. It was known that Jan Vriesman loved to smoke cigars. When the German captain came in the house, he asked whether there were any males in the house and Marjanne's stepmother said no, that her husband had gone on a business trip. Suddenly another member of the household, a woman, saw a cigar in the ashtray, which was luckily not lit. She was able to grab the cigar before the Germans saw it, and the story is that she ate it, to keep them from finding it.

The German captain, who it turned out was not really in agreement with the Nazis on these tactics, talked to Marjanne's stepmother in a nice way. He knew there was really nobody on a business trip, and while the soldiers went quickly through the house, he showed her pictures of his own wife and children back in Germany and he apologized for having to search the house. The soldiers went down to the lowest level toward the platform that led to the water, and it was dark and shadowy down there. Instead of really searching, they just looked down into the hole and no one wanted to go any farther, so they said, "Oh, there's nothing down here, let's go." Of course, that's where Vriesman was hiding.

Vriesman managed to move around enough through the rest of the war to avoid being found, but he must have been underground for at least two years.

Saving the babies

Marjanne's mother, Elizabeth Schneyder, or Omie as we called her, lived in Noordwijk, which was on the sea, north and west of Dordrecht. My daughter, Jennifer, talked with her grandmother in 1994 when Omie was in her 80s, about another story involving Jewish babies. There are many versions of the story about the babies, and it was believed it happened while the Schneyders were living at their home called Ashlar in the city of Noordwijk, but here is Omie's story in Jennifer's words:

> Actually, the passing of the babies did not occur at Ashlar, rather it was in Amsterdam in the early 1940s. Omie and Opie (Elizabeth and Bart Schneyder) had been displaced from their home after the Nazis had taken Ashlar to use as a "watch" over the ocean where they believed the Americans would come. They were moved by the Nazis to Amsterdam during this time, and the house was given back to them after the war.
>
> One day Omie came around a corner in Amsterdam and saw many people being rounded up at gunpoint. Suddenly a man came running from an alley and handed her a baby explaining someone would come to her for the baby. The

man was subsequently chased down and taken away. Omie rushed home with the baby not knowing what to do, but she took care of it. In the middle of that night, there was a knock at the door and someone did come for the baby to take it to safety. Omie handed the baby over and never knew what became of it. In the weeks to follow, she said several more babies came through her door and the same process occurred. She did not ask questions. She believed she was able to get away with it because she was a Dutch woman who was fluent in German.

There were many other stories about her going over the border into Germany and people hiding under the floor boards of Ashlar before it was taken. She told me these stories with a lot more details on two separate occasions years apart, so I have a propensity to believe her account.

After the "interrogation"

Unfortunately, after returning to school following what I will forever remember as "the interrogation," I learned during the following two years I really didn't like mechanical engineering. It was dirty work and I didn't like getting my hands dirty, and it smelled bad, too. At the end of my second year, I decided to switch majors. Of course, I must add that my professors might have played a role in that decision. In fact, one of them, a quiet man of intense integrity, for some reason must have sensed my aversion to my chosen field. During a test one day, he laid his hand on the test on my desk and said in a calm voice, "As long as I am a professor in this school, I will see to it that you will *never* become a mechanical engineer."

I can never underestimate the long reach of my father. I'm positive he had a role in the head of the school approaching me to do some psychological testing to see what discipline might work better for me than mechanical engineering. In any case, I did the testing and it was determined I would better succeed in electrical engineering, and this became my new goal. We all knew I was open for the draft because of my decision to change majors, and this nice man who headed the school told me when I was finished with my military service, there would be a spot saved for me in the HTS Dordrecht electrical engineering department.

In Holland, there was an extension for the draft as long as you were pursuing your major in college. However, because I had announced my intention of switching majors, I was open to the draft, and sure enough, at the bureaucratic request of the Queen, before I could start on my new studies, I was summoned to Her Majesty's Royal Dutch Army.

Her Majesty's Royal Dutch Army

I went by train and reported for duty in Amsterdam. Basic training was okay, but I didn't like the marching. For some reason the army decided I should become a sergeant and after training they sent me to sergeant school. Apparently I did not do well in sergeant school because they decided I "lacked military posture," and sent me back for reassignment. Relieved, because I didn't really like sergeant school, I was sent back to Amsterdam where I was asked what I wanted to do. On the spur of the moment I said I wanted to be a truck driver, thinking this might not be a bad thing to do. This idea was well received and away I went to truck driver training.

I drove a big truck that hauled gasoline in jerry-cans, five-gallon square containers. Of course, there was always a machine gun turret for a .50 caliber machine gun on the truck "just in case," because in times of war these trucks might be hauling supplies to the front line and they needed to be armed. We always had an assistant driver, too, who was usually a new recruit. He also had the job of helping the other recruits load and unload when we got to our destinations, and that was one of the perks in being the driver – I didn't have to load and unload. Drivers were not allowed to perform manual labor, right up my alley.

One day I needed to hitch a ride back to the base and rode with another driver and his assistant. The engines in these trucks were in the center between the driver and the passenger seat, and were covered with a metal box. I found it odd that whenever they approached a corner, this driver would nod to his assistant, who would move to sit on the center box and both of them would move the steering wheel. One pulled and the other pushed. I asked questions about this practice and the driver said he couldn't handle it by himself. I thought, "What a weakling this guy is!" and said I'd like to try it myself.

The driver said, "Go ahead and try it!" and I got in the driver's seat. We were going slowly into a small village on a straight stretch and I had no problems. Ahead I could see there was a T in the road with a bakery nearby. I knew we had to make a left turn by the bakery and I reduced speed even more by using the pneumatic brakes that went "whoosh whoosh." I began to make the turn and suddenly realized there was no power steering. Using every bit of strength I had, I could barely move the steering wheel at all. I kept on hitting the brakes, whooshing all the way, and we finally stopped about three inches from the bakery window. People on the inside of the store were frozen and clutching donuts about the same size as their eyes when they saw this huge truck bearing down on them.

I meekly admitted to the first driver that now I understood why it took two of them to turn the truck. Apparently it was taking the army a while to fix his power steering and they were making do as best they could. I was happy to get back to my own truck which had its power steering intact.

I met a guy in the army who was my assistant driver for a while. He was a big handsome Dutch fellow, only about 17 years old, and strong as a bull. His name was Tromp, and he told me he was a bricklayer before the army, building streets. He worked on his knees leveling the sand and laying bricks every day. He made really good money at this and he planned to return to it after the army because his contractor agreed to take him back. I asked what he was going to do after that. He said, "What do you mean after that? I'll be laying bricks!"

I realized this man planned to lay bricks for the rest of his life. All I could think was how it would be to be 55 years old, with creaky knees and maybe some arthritis or something, and have to crawl around on my knees all day laying bricks. This was an "aha moment" for me and I knew for certain how lucky I was to be going back to college to prepare for a life where I didn't have to lay bricks, or hopefully, even have to fight with power steering.

One day I was approached by my captain, the company commander, who asked if I would like to become the private driver for the colonel. This was definitely something I wanted to do, and I took the job for several months. I drove a Volkswagen – one of the earlier Beetles, and took the colonel wherever he wanted to go. Of course, by fudging the paperwork I could use the car to go to the movies now and then, which was a bonus.

However, I found out later this job would require me to stay in Her Majesty's Army for extra time, which I didn't want to do. I was called in to see another colonel who told me this, and I said no one had told me I had to stay in, and I'd rather get out in the original 18 months I had been assigned. He was not happy about this at all and amid much red-faced cussing and swearing when finding out somebody goofed in not telling me, he made several loud phone calls. The result was that I had to petition to get out after 18 months so I could take the tutoring required for me to change my major in college.

I made it through the petitioning and gratefully went back to college before I was actually discharged from the army. In addition, I continued to get my pittance of pay until I was discharged about four months later, plus an additional small amount because I lived off the base. I stayed a short time with my mother in The Hague, and then went back to Dordrecht and stayed with the van Slootens again.

I was in the logistics division of the army when I was driving trucks, and years later when I worked for 3M in the U.S., I spent most of my career in logistics. I didn't drive trucks, but maybe in my heart of hearts, I missed the excitement of it all.

Same school, new major

I didn't realize what a gift I had been given in having a seat saved for me at school after the army. I learned later there were many students who would have loved my spot. Oblivious to it all, I returned to Dordrecht with renewed enthusiasm in tackling my studies. The two years of college before my time in the army were completely disregarded and I had to start over from scratch. This didn't feel like a burden with my keenness to accomplish my new goal. The tutoring was a big help, and the professor said I would do well in my classes, which I did. I liked the electrical engineering teaching staff better, and the topics covered were more logical to me. I was certainly more motivated, and that carried through my whole undergraduate time.

I stayed with the van Slootens through my first two years of study in my new field. The third year at HTS was considered a training or practice year, and we were sent to work in companies in the area on a sort of intern program. I started out in Dordrecht and then went to The Hague, and then to the Philips Company in Eindhoven for three months, working with electronics. From there I went to Germany and worked for another three months with the Siemens Company in Berlin.

Berlin

Living in Berlin was fascinating because the city was like an island, surrounded by the Communists. I was there with two other students and we stayed in a boarding house in West Berlin within walking distance of Siemens. We could walk around and go in and out of East Berlin with no problem, but we were not allowed to go into East Germany.

East and West Berlin were as different as night and day. West

Berlin was a booming and thriving business community with restored and rebuilt buildings and businesses, restaurants and an active night life. East Berlin was a depressing gray pile of rubble with barbed wire and soldiers halting any access to East Germany. We saw few people and those wore sad expressions and looked constantly harried.

The aftermath of war was evident everywhere we went. The people, especially men, were either very old or very young. There were few of middle age and many were obviously damaged by the war, with missing limbs, or blind, or impaired in some way. I worked in the relay department of Siemens assembling relay switches, and most of the other people working there were physically impaired, many of them blind. Because of this, and my being physically whole, I was amazingly efficient at turning out relay switches, and continually exceeded my quotas. Eventually, I was approached by other workers and told to slow down because I was making them look bad. I have to say this was the first – and last – time I was ever reprimanded for being too fast!

My faith life

As I have said, our family was Christian. We never attended church regularly, but my mother had always read us many stories from the Bible and prayer was a constant. I learned about the Bible heroes, including Samson and David, John the Baptist, and Jesus, of course, and others.

My father had been raised Catholic, and my mother was Dutch Reform Protestant. When they married, it was not acceptable for a Catholic to marry out of the faith. My mother also refused to have her children baptized Roman Catholic, so my father was excommunicated from the church. Neither of them were church-goers, so it didn't really affect our family very much. However, when Huibert was born, he had some medical issues that caused him to have seizures. This was terribly frightening to my parents, and my mother agreed that Huibert could be baptized into the Roman Catholic Church, fearfully thinking they were being punished for something. The seizures eventually went away and I was born without those problems.

Then the war started and my father was taken off to POW camp. Well into the war my mother must have drawn closer to her religious upbringing, and she had me baptized in the Dutch Reform Protestant Church which was not far from our home. I was eight or nine years old. We still did not regularly attend church, but it must have eased her mind that I was baptized.

Throughout our years in Indonesia we never did attend church, and we didn't go to church when we were in Holland either. In Huibert's later life he was drawn back to the Roman Catholic faith and has been a faithful church member for many years. His second wife, Judy, is also Catholic and they have always done a great deal of volunteer work with the church.

I, on the other hand, began to have serious doubts about religion and faith itself when I went to college. We had always prayed in our house, led by my mother, and as I said, I knew the Bible stories, but I had doubts. As an engineer, there were some things that were just not logical to me and I was wrestling with my basic belief in God. Is He real, or is He not? I had trouble believing the stories I learned as a child.

One of the stories had to do with Samson, the strong man who supposedly collapsed the pagan Gaza Temple. It was the material strength theory of forces that brought about both my disbelief, and ultimately, my absolute belief in the Bible. In other words, science led me away from God, and science brought me back.

When I first started college in my mechanical engineering days, I was wrestling with the reality of God. In fact, I spent many sleepless nights wondering and questioning my beliefs. The more I thought about it, the crazier it was. Soon an amazing new and exciting movie, Cecil B. DeMille's "Samson and Delilah" captured the world's attention. I saw the movie sometime in 1954, and I was mesmerized by Samson and his incredible strength. I was appalled watching him be tortured and kept in chains. The story was true to the Bible as I knew it, and in fascination I watched Samson stand between the huge columns of the temple, and press outward with his arms.

Watching the scene of Samson's arms that looked like matchsticks compared to the enormous size of the columns, I knew from what I had learned so far of science, it was not technically possible for him to break the columns. His arms would shatter before the columns could even bend. There was no logical way this could be done, and I concluded immediately the Bible was all nonsense.

It was a huge load off my shoulders, and I no longer struggled with my beliefs. I decided then and there the stories were false, and therefore there was no God. My life from that point on was immensely more comfortable because I no longer wondered. In my mind, science proved it.

However, my smug self-righteousness was in for a blessed awakening.

In my last year of college, there came a professor, a younger man who was Dutch, but he had darker skin and eyes so black they sparkled. He had a full black beard, pearly white teeth, a head of wild unkempt hair, and a demeanor of excitement about him that was captivating. He looked exactly as my mind pictured John the Baptist.

He was teaching an advanced course of material strength and on this particular day I sat in the front row. I was directly in line with his spittle as he stormed around the room expounding on the theories and the formulas involved in determining how strong something might be. He explained and gave examples of what formulas are needed to make something break or buckle. The middle is the weak spot of a vertically positioned bar which is under pressure of opposite forces, because the forces meet in the middle of the bar. The forces generate heat in the middle of the bar and can soften the material. Depending on the amount of pressure, this can allow the bar to buckle, with little or no horizontal pressure needed.

He suddenly twirled around in front of the room and his black eyes focused solidly on mine, as he clearly cried out, "And yes, gentlemen, this also holds true for temple columns!"

Eureka! The scene of Samson standing between the enormous temple columns and pressing with his arms came to my mind in a flash. I had been hit by a boulder. I knew with complete assurance the story of Samson was *true*. He did push those columns and destroy the temple, just as the Bible said. The weight on the columns created heat, and science proved Samson could destroy them!

A feeling washed over me that I can only describe as an emotional reawakening. I lost my breath and gasped for air. I felt a certainty, a confidence, and a conviction that all I had learned about the Bible was true. And this amazing born-again feeling has stayed with me from that moment to this. Never again has my faith waivered. God was with me through all the years of my doubt and my searching, and He will be with me forever.

Eviction

While Indonesia was officially recognized as an independent nation in 1949, things didn't change overnight. My father and Jan Bartels were able to operate their businesses without much intervention. However, an edict came from the Indonesian government announcing 51 percent of all European-owned businesses had to be owned by full Indonesian people. There was no way around it, and no money was allowed to leave the country either. My father approached a local native Javanese small businessman he knew who was called "Soes." He was an honest man who was trustworthy, and Pa said to him, "Soes, you now own 51 percent of my businesses." Soes argued and said, "But I don't have any money. I can't buy into your businesses."

Pa told him not to worry, they would work things out. They obviously came to some agreement and my father worked out a system by which he could have some of his commissions paid overseas.

From the time of Indonesia's independence in 1949 to as late as the mid-1960s, there were several "waves" of Dutch and Indo people leaving the country. People of Dutch citizenship were deemed "undesired elements" by the young republic of Indonesia, and the government eventually demanded 100 percent ownership of all business by Indonesian citizens. Indos were forced to give up their Dutch citizenship and assume Indonesian citizenship, or leave the country. Sources say[13] that up to 10 percent of the remaining Dutch and Indos in the country accepted Indonesian citizenship, but I think this number is high.

Thousands of Indos left Indonesia for other countries, including Holland, the U.S., Australia, and all over the world. They are assimilating into their host societies, and it is a sad fact that with age and intermarriage, Indos are now disappearing as a group.[14]

I left for college in Holland in 1953. Not long after that, my father left on a trip to see where in the world he might want to live and start a new business. He went to several European countries, the U.S. – even bringing along a car and traveling through the country – and Australia and New Guinea. While in New Guinea in 1956 he received a telegram from Bartels saying he should not return to Bandung. The Indonesian government was confiscating all non-Indonesian-owned business and they were being forced out of the country. Bartels offered to close down the businesses and pack up their houses and as many household goods as he was able to take out of the country. This was a huge job and I will be forever grateful to Jan and Oije for helping my family.

My mother also left Indonesia in 1956. She had been living and working at the hotel owned by my friend Cor Schalks' father. Mother went to The Hague, in Holland, where she worked for a number of years in a government job. Two of her sisters eventually joined her there, and I visited her many times. Her asthma was better treated in Holland and she lived a comfortable life until she died of cancer in 1968.

My father and An relocated to Holland for several years. He started a new business with his old companion, Jan Bartels, a

[13] R. B. Cribb, Audrey Kahin, Historical Dictionary of Indonesia, 2004, p. 185.
[14] David Levinson, Melvin Ember, American immigrant cultures: builders of a nation, 1997, p. 441.

dealership for Audi automobiles in Breda. They sold the business in 1962, and Pa and An went to the U.S., settling in Texas. He worked with a friend's Harley Davidson dealership there and was put in charge of developing the golf cart business, a new branch of Harley Davidson. This started a new passion for playing golf which he thoroughly enjoyed. Sadly, my father was hit by a car and never fully recovered from the accident. Pa died in 1979.

Whirlwind exodus

When I returned to Dordrecht for my last year of college, I kept my nose to the grindstone and studied hard. I was 25 years old and determined to be successful with my final examinations. I was also determined I was not going to live in Holland. I had looked long and hard at other places in the world where I wanted to live, including Australia and Canada (closed to people born in Asian countries), or Rhodesia, South Africa, and Argentina (Pa said these would all be like Indonesia). I settled on the United States because of the freedoms offered and my overall admiration for Americans. (There was a 12-year wait for Indonesian quotas for immigration to the U.S., but I had hopes for being accepted by the Pastore-Walter Immigration Act.)

I applied for immigration through the Pastore-Walter Immigration Act when it was extended early in 1960 and was hopeful but didn't yet have my acceptance.

From Wikipedia®: The 1953 flood disaster in the Netherlands (a combination of high spring tides and a severe European wind storm over the North Sea that flooded and ruined hundreds of farms and villages) resulted in the Refugee Relief Act including a slot for 15,000 ethnic Dutch who had at least 50 percent European blood and an immaculate legal and political track record. In 1954 only 187 visas were actually granted. Partly influenced by the anti-Western rhetoric and policies of the Sukarno administration, the anti-communist senator Francis E. Walter pleaded for a second term of the Refugee Relief Act in 1957. In 1958 the Pastore-Walter Immigration Act (Act for the relief of certain distressed aliens) was passed allowing for acceptance of 10,000 Dutchmen from Indonesia. In 1960 senators Pastore and Walter managed to get a second two-year term for their act which was used by a great number of Dutch Indos.

After the time of my "conversion" or my reawakening to God's presence in my life, I began to talk to Him often in my mind. In fact, some of these conversations were quite lively. For example, one night I was "bargaining" with God, and telling Him, "I really hope you could help me succeed in passing my examinations, and by the way, in a couple of years I would like to move to the United States. The people in Holland are wonderful, but the climate is so politically oppressive and besides it's so cold all the time. I just don't like it here." Then I finished up with, "And if you can help me with all that, I do promise I will go to church when I get there."

I swear I heard the Almighty say, "Okay!"

The first success was miraculously passing my final college examinations – a grueling period which lasted from mid-June through mid-July, with results received in late July 1961. I graduated with a Bachelor of Science degree in electrical engineering, and it was a thrilling day.

I neglected to say the Almighty added a postscript in His answer to my lengthy bargaining discussion. It was, "If you're going all the way to the U.S., then you'd better bring someone along with you. And here she is!"

"She," was Marjanne Vriesman, my long-time friend who stole my heart when she agreed to go with me to the United States to start a new life together.

Marjanne and I had been friends, along with her sisters and several others, through my college years when I first boarded with the van Slootens. Through the years our friendship turned to love, and with excitement we planned our future in a new country.

During the busy time of my college examinations I received word that I had been accepted for immigration to the United States, and Marjanne as my wife would also be accepted. We were sponsored by the World Church Organization along with my brother Huibert, who was already in the U.S. and going to school in Minnesota. With the blessings of our families, which required much discussion and persuasion on the part of Marjanne's father especially, we were married on August 18, 1961.

In a whirlwind exodus, before the end of September 1961, with eager anticipation of a new life in America, we boarded a Constellation airplane headed for LaGuardia Airport, New York, U.S.A. We were on our way to a new life and a new paradise.

Epilogue

We boarded the plane in Amsterdam in September 1961. We dressed for the occasion with me in a heavy suit, and Marjanne in a woolen tweed skirt suit, complete with hat and long white gloves. Upon landing in New York, the temperature was 105 degrees. By the time we stepped off the plane, her hat was tilted and we were both thoroughly wilted. But our enthusiasm was strong and we were finally in America!

I have to reiterate my thanks to the American people for your sacrifices in winning World War II. This is something deep in my heart for which I will always be grateful. You saved the lives of my whole family, and those of millions of others.

After open-mouth sight-seeing in New York City for several days, we boarded a train that raced across the continent with a dizzying display of incredible openness. There were trees and more trees, fields of corn and other crops, and vast areas of nothing – unimaginable in Holland, where every square foot of land is used for something. In actuality, Holland is one-seventh the size of Minnesota, and currently has more than twice as many people. The vastness across the U.S. was overwhelming.

Our plan was to stay briefly in Minnesota and go on from there to California, where the weather is warmer. However, we had family in Minnesota and our sponsors, also. In addition, the sun seemed to shine every day and in spite of the cold winter, the sun made all the difference. I decided to look for work. After applying at several companies, Huibert told me about 3M, or Minnesota Mining and

Manufacturing as it was called in those days. When I went for an interview, I was instantly struck by the friendliness of the company, and when they offered me a job, I decided this was the place for me. The feeling was mutual, and after 35 years of satisfying and fulfilling work in logistics with 3M, I retired in 1996.

Marjanne and I had a good life together and we had two children, Mark and Jennifer. We built a lovely home near Lake Jane in Lake Elmo, and enjoyed playing tennis with many friends. We became naturalized U.S. citizens in 1967 after taking classes in culture, history, and how the government works, giving us a deeper insight to the country.

Remembering my covenant with God and my promise to attend a church, we began to look at many area churches. We were encouraged by neighbors to visit Christ Lutheran in Lake Elmo, and we felt immediately at home there and joined the congregation.

After a number of years, Marjanne began exhibiting the symptoms of a debilitating disease that had no cure. Sadly, she passed away in early 2003.

Another member of our church, Gloria Cannon, lost her husband to cancer a few months before Marjanne died. Actually, Marjanne and Gene Cannon were on hospice care at the same time and were talking weekly on the phone with each other through the summer of 2002. We didn't really know each other very well, and Gloria and I never did meet or talk to one another during that time, but they enjoyed their conversations.

I went to Holland to visit family after Marjanne's death. When the time came to go home, I had another conversation with God. I told him I didn't know what I wanted, but I didn't want to grow old alone, and would He please find just the right woman for me. I said it would probably take a while but could He do it in two years or so, which I thought was reasonable. I left Holland for home, and two weeks later Gloria and I met at church. This was the first of September 2003, and sparks must have flown because we were married in January 2004.

Gloria and I have been together more than 10 years now and we are loving life together, whether it's traveling, playing at tennis, or visiting with friends. We've even got a small group of local Indo friends we see regularly. We are both hospice volunteers, too, in thanks for the wonderful care provided to our former spouses. Combined, we have 8 children plus mates, 21 grandchildren, 7 great-grandchildren at this point, and many nieces and nephews, so life is never dull. We are grateful for a loving God who guides us every step of the way and continues to bless us. We cherish every day we have together.

It's been 53 years now that I've lived in Minnesota. I'm still on my way to California.

Glossary

Dutch and Indonesian words/terms

Babu: servant

Bak: box

Batik: fabric that is covered with wax dots and lines before dyeing

Baying: shadow

Bersiap: get ready or be prepared. Also the violent and chaotic phase of the Indonesian National Revolution following the end of World War II.

Besar: big

Dennelust: pine tree delight

Djarak: the castor plant, which produces castor oil

Dokar: horse-drawn cart

Dukun: a witch doctor

Gado gado: Indonesian salad

Gajah Merah: The Indonesian phrase literally means "red elephant." It was a special division of the Dutch East Indies Army known to be fierce fighters.

Gamel: mallet used to strike a musical instrument

Gamelan: The overall term for an orchestra composed of instruments including metallic drums of various sizes which are struck with a mallet creating a "gong" sound.

Gurkas: Mongolian Buddhist people

Hongerwinter: Hunger Winter

Indo: person of mixed Indonesian and European heritage

Kampong: local native village

Katte: cats

Kempeitai: the military police arm of the Imperial Japanese Army – a much feared secret police group.

Ketjiel: small

Koffie toebroek: strong coffee

Kokkie: cook

Kraton: palace

Merdeka: freedom

Maling: thief

Nasi goring: fried rice

Oom: Uncle

Oma: Grandmother

Opa: Grandfather

Pakjesavond: packages evening

Panser wagens: armored trucks

Patat friet: French fries

Pemuda: youth troops

Put: open well

Rijsttafel: rice table, or an elaborate meal

Sambal: hot pepper sauce

Sarong: native skirt

Satay: a dish of skewered and grilled meat served with sauce

Sawa: rice field

Shu: sauce or gravy

Sinterklaas: Santa Claus

Sinterklaasavond: gifts evening

Tangkuban Perahu: upturned boat

Tante: Aunt

Wayang: generic term for Indonesian puppetry theater

Wayang golek: three-dimensional wooden puppets

Wayang kulit: shadow puppets

Wayang orang: real people playing the roles of wayang

Weltevreden: satisfied

Voor en Door Ons: For and By Us, shortened to Vedo, the name of my high school student club

Zwarte Piet: Black Pete is the controversial servant of Sinterklaas. Some say he got his name because he carried the gifts down the chimneys and his face was black from soot. Others say he was a Moor, a dark-skinned man from Spain or North Africa.

References

Books, Reports, and Web Pages

"American immigrant cultures: builders of a nation," David Levinson, Melvin Ember, 1997, p. 441.

"Center for Research, Allied POWs Under the Japanese." Site for the detailed study of all Allied POWs of the Japanese during World War II. Roger Mansell, founder, with work continued by Wes Injerd.

Duffy, George and Australian Dr. van Ramshorst, from the website by John Winterbotham: www.australian-pow-ww2.com/sumatra_17.html

"Dutch Patronymics of the 1600s," Lorine McGinnis Schulze, (2008-03-04). *New Netherland, New York Genealogy.* Olive Tree Genealogy.

"Historical Dictionary of Indonesia," R. B. Cribb, Audrey Kahin, 2004, p. 185.

"History Today" Volume: 49, Issue 11 1999. Dean Nicholas, Website manager, History Today

"Nederlands-Indie 1940-1950 In Kort Bestek." Sjoerd A. Lapré, RMWO.

"Rising from the Shadow of the Sun, A story of Love, Survival and Joy," by Ronny Herman de Jong, BookLocker.com, Inc., 2011, First Edition.

"We Band of Angels: The Untold Story of the American Women Trapped on Bataan," by Elizabeth Norman, Random House Trade Paperbacks Reprint edition, 2013.

Wikipedia®, the Internet's free encyclopedia. http://en.wikipedia.org/wiki/Main_Page

About the Author

Describing her own life experiences in a unique way, Gloria VanDemmeltraadt's first book, *Musing and Munching*, is both a memoir and a cook book. Her work is focused on drawing out precious memories. As a hospice volunteer, she continues to hone her gift for capturing life stories and refined this gift in *Memories of Lake Elmo*, a collection of remembrances telling the evolving story of a charming village.

Gloria continues her passion to help people capture their life stories, and has now brilliantly caught the essence of her husband's early life in war-torn Indonesia. The paradise of the Dutch East Indies was shattered when Japanese storm troopers poured over the island of Java in March 1942. In *Darkness in Paradise*, Onno VanDemmeltraadt's story is touchingly told amid the horrors of war.

Gloria and Onno VanDemmeltraadt live in Oakdale, MN.

Contact Gloria through her website: gloriavan.com